IN THE SHADOW OF THE BLACKDOWNS

J. A. SPARKS

IN THE SHADOW OF THE BLACKDOWNS

Life at the Cistercian Abbey of Dunkeswell
and on its Manors and Estates
1201—1539

MOONRAKER PRESS

First published in 1978 by Moonraker Press
26 St Margarets Street, Bradford-on-Avon, Wiltshire
SBN 239.00178.8
Text set in 11/13 pt Photon Times, printed by photolithography, and bound
in Great Britain at The Pitman Press, Bath.

Contents

Preface

THE BLACKDOWNS provide a magnificent view of the countryside of eastern Devon and from their lofty eminence have looked down upon countless generations of people who, since the dawn of history, have wrested a livelihood from the land which stretches as far as the eye can see into the heartland of Devon. They form a natural boundary between the counties of Devon and Somerset. Long before men lived upon their slopes this was wild hunting-country and the home of the wolf.

When the Romans came they built a road along the crest of the range and called it Ford Street. In the eighth century it was the boundary between the West Saxons and the native Dumnonians, and upon its summit the famous King Ina of the West Saxons fought his last battle against Dumnonia about the year A.D. 710, when the boundary between Wessex and Dumnonia was fixed along the ridge of the Blackdowns. On the east-Devon side of the ridge a large barrow or tumulus was constructed with a base area of about one acre. Legend has it that it was erected over the grave of one Simon the overlord of Exmoor who perished in the battle against the West Saxons: having regard to its size it might well have been the burial place of the native Dumnonians who fell in that battle. The tumulus has long been known as Simonsbarrow. The grave is believed to have been opened sometime in the 18th century.

With the coming of the Normans in 1066 the Conqueror gave special permission to a branch of the Hidon family of Clayhidon to erect a Castle at Hemyock which was then a Royal desmesne lying in the valley at the foot of the hill. The Castle was occupied and used for centuries but at the restoration in 1660 it was demolished for supporting the Parliamentary cause in the Civil War, when the Castle was used as a prison. Only fragments of it now remain.

It was the coming of the Cistercians to Dunkeswell in 1201 that brought an entirely new dimension to the life of society in the eastern region of Devon. In the shadow of the Blackdowns the Cistercians acquired much land and developed their Manor and Grange farms, and over a very wide area the Abbots of Dunkeswell exercised judicial powers for the keeping of the King's Peace and the regulation of the price and quality of corn, ale and bread. After

338 years of existence the Cisterians brought about great changes in agriculture and the way of life of a large number of people whose livelihood was bound up with the soil.

In the year 1817 a monumental pillar containing 365 steps was erected on the summit of the Blackdowns in honour of the Duke of Wellington who defeated Napoleon at the decisive battle of Waterloo. The Monument can be seen for many miles around and is a prominent feature of the landscape. The Cistercians, however, had long since departed and the stones of their Abbey had been taken to build many a farm-building and cottage scattered over the landscape in the shadow of the Blackdowns.

The emphasise in this book is upon the 13th- and 14th-century activities of the Cistercian community when it was an active, energetic and progressive force in medieval society. With the disappearance of the Conversi after the Black Death in 1348, whose labour on farm, field and wasteland contributed so much to the Cistercian achievement, the community became static and conservative and impervious to the need for change and reform, particularly in its temporal responsibilities. The Cistercians retreated deeper into the spiritual life and left their Manors and estates in the hands of paid bailiffs, stewards and servants who managed them in the style of the private landowner. Their isolation produced an indifference to the world outside and to the growing demand within the Church itself for reform and change in their conduct and behaviour, until finally the Reformation overwhelmed them and swept them away. There was much in monasticism that was good and many Houses with blameless records and behaviour went down with the disorderly and corrupt in the dissolution of 1539.

The Cistercians were at Dunkeswell for 338 years and they left their mark upon medieval life over a very wide area of Eastern Devon.

With acknowledgements to the British Library for permitting the reproduction of drawings that are partly based on manuscripts in its collection and to the Devon Record Office and the Devon and Cornwall Record Society for some items included from their records.

J. A. SPARKS

CHAPTER ONE

The Foundation of Dunkeswell Abbey

Foundation of Dunkeswell Abbey: Forde Abbey – Lord William Brewer – his Charter. Monks from Forde arrive – local peasants give their land. Construction begins – King John's Charter 1206. The Lady Chapel nears completion – visit of the Archbishop of Canterbury 1225 – the Founder's burial place. The east range – south range – west range – The Nave of the Church. Home farm – fishponds – the mill – gatehouse – school house – the cloister.

IT IS recorded in the Annales of Margam Abbey for the year 1201 that on August 15 of that year at Forde Abbey (near Chard), the Convent was assembled to select 12 Monks who, with the workman Gregory at their head, were to build the Abbey of Dunekeswille. At this ceremony were also present John, Abbot of Waverley, John, Abbot of Forde and Lord William Brewer. The presence of the Abbot of Waverley, the Mother Abbey of the Order in England, indicates the great importance of the occasion for the Cistercians. This event followed the granting of a Charter by William Brewer, an abstract of which is preserved in the early records of the Duchy of Lancaster as follows:

To all Christ's faithful to whom (the present deed shall come), William Brewer, greeting. Know all of you that I, for the salvation of the souls of my Lords Henry and Richard, Kings of England, and the souls of my father and mother, and my soul and those of Beatrice, my wife, and my children and all my ancestors and successors, have given and granted to God, (and Blessed) Mary and the Cistercian Order all my lands of Donkewell and of Wulferchurch with the advowson of the Churches of the aforesaid lands, and all their appurtenances, in free, pure and perpetual alms, quit of all services and secular exactions, to build an Abbey of the aforesaid Order in the aforesaid Manor of Donkewell from the Convent of Forde. And so that my gift and grant may remain firm for ever I have corroborated it with the present deed and the appending of my seal. These are witnesses. . . .

(P.R.O. DL/36/3, Folio 92. No. 221).

The founder, Lord William Brewer, was a distinguished man of his times and the confidante of Kings. He was Sheriff of Devon 1179–89, a Judge in the reign of Richard I (1189–99) and one of the triumvirate who ruled England during Richard's absence on a Crusade to the Holy Land. Later he became Sheriff of Cornwall 1202–3 and Sheriff of Dorset and Somerset in 1209. He was a reluctant signatory of Magna Carta in 1215 and had founded other Religious Houses. On 28 October 1224 in the presence of the King at Westminster he

1

gave up all the lands he held of the King in Chief and the King accepted the homage of his son William. He then retired to the Abbey at Dunkeswell where he became a Lay Brother of the Cistercians sometime before his death which occurred on 24 November 1226. The founder was buried before the Great Altar in the Lady Chapel of the Conventual Church. His son William survived his father by only seven years and was buried before the Great Altar of the Premonstratensian Abbey of Torre which was founded by his father in 1196 and, dying childless, he left a substantial estate at Buckland Brewer to the Abbey at Dunkeswell.

Upon the small body of Monks from Forde Abbey and the workman Gregory fell the formidable task of erecting the new Abbey at Dunkeswell. Sited in a valley in the foothills of the Blackdown Hills, through which the Madford River winds its way to join the Culme at Hemyock, it is sheltered on all sides by high ridges; on the west by Collards Hill and on the east by Abbey Hill. At the confluence of the Madford River and a tributary stream on the west, which fed two large fishponds, the foundations of the Abbey were laid. Nearby, William Brewer had a house or enclosure – probably a hunting lodge and kennels – known as Brewerhayes but later corrupted to Bowerhayes. There is little doubt that he selected the site of the Abbey and that the Diocesan and the General Chapter of the Cistercian Order approved.

It was on 16 November in the year 1201 that the small party of 12 monks from the Cistercian Abbey of Forde, with the workman Gregory and carrying their cross before them, arrived upon the site of Dunkeswell Abbey. They were received by the founder and a gathering of local people. The founder conducted them to the site which they entered in solemn procession chanting the *Salve Regina* – a hymn or prayer to the Virgin Mary. They were introduced to a group of temporary wooden structures roofed with thatch comprising a Chapel, a place for eating and sleeping, a house for guests and a porter's lodge at the entry to the site. William was their first Abbot and was so named after the founder as was the usual custom, while the community appointed from among themselves a Prior, sub-Prior, Sacrist, Cellarer, Precentor and a porter for the lodge who was a lay brother. There were two great tasks before them – the building of permanent structures and the organisation of supplies of food and the necessities of life for the community. They were settled in a remote and isolated spot which called for great qualities of endurance in the long winter months of cold and wet. Very soon after their arrival gifts of land were made to them by small peasants in the locality who, finding life hard and insecure, made over their land to the Abbey in return for a carrody in which the Abbot and the Monks undertook to provide food, clothing and shelter and security for themselves and their families for life. Some of these peasants joined the community as *conversi* and others as servants, and in due time their sons followed them into the service of the Abbey. In this way a nucleus labour-force was created to cultivate and develop the land around the Abbey to provide the home farm upon which the community could secure its food supplies and commence erection of the Abbey structures.

A group of craftsmen who had special permission to move around the country on construction work was assisted by the monks and any local labour that could be got. In charge of construction was a master mason who was something of a working architect and he was appointed by the founder and the Abbot to take charge of the work. The plan and design of construction was agreed by them and this conformed to the 13th-century Cistercian Plan with which the master mason would have been familiar. This plan was less severe and austere than earlier plans though simple and graceful in style, and the craftsmen would have been selected for their experience in the construction of Cistercian Houses. The master mason appointed his assistant to supervise the work of the masons, carpenters and others from local sources who did the digging and carting away. The pay of the Master mason was about 10p a day and if the job was a long one he expected to be provided with a house. His assistant received about 15p a week and the rest about 12½p a week downwards. The monks received no pay for the contribution they made.

The cost involved in the building-programme must have been considerable and there is no doubt that the founder made the largest contribution, but there were other more modest people who gave land and its revenues to the newly established convent. In addition to the gifts of William Brewer, the Abbot of Forde and Ursus son of William gave their land at nearby Bywood (Dunkeswell). Richard of Hidon gave about 30 acres of nearby land at Bowerhayes and Richard of Treminetes and William of Pinu gave their lands at Bantesnappe (Dunkeswell). John of Treiton gave about eight acres of land at nearby Stentwood and Yvonis son of Allan gave his Manor of Sobbecombe (Luppitt) which Manor at the time of the Doomsday survey consisted of 120 acres of ploughland of which the Lord ploughed 37½ acres with one plough and his three villeins ploughed 82¾ acres with one plough. There was one bordar, one serf, 20 acres of woods, 12 acres of meadow and 15 acres of pasture in the Manor which was worth for tax purposes £1 a year. Richard of Manelega gave a tenement in Marlcombe (Auliscombe). Philip of Gatiden gave about eight acres of land in Uggaton and Robert son of Amicia, and Ursus son of William, each gave a tenement in Lynor (Hackpen). The grants and revenues were confirmed in King John's Charter 13 April 1206 in which he also said:

Know all of you that the said Monks of Dunkeswell may have and hold the said tenements and everything belonging to them well and in peace – in perpetuity. Know you also that we have taken the said Monks of Dunkeswell and all their men, lands and tenements and other things and have placed their possessions under our guard, protection and care forbidding under pain of forfeiture anyone to do them any hurt, injury or wrong . . .

This Charter was witnessed by six distinguished men and Hugh, Archdeacon of Wells.

William Brewer added to his original gifts to the Abbey the large Manor of Hembury (Broadhembury) sometime between the years 1206 and 1217, and shortly after this lands in the Manor of Collaton (Collaton Raleigh) and land in the Manor of Uffculme, with the mill. Nearer the time of his death in 1226 he added what appears to be his last gift of the Manor of Lincombe (Ilfracombe). These gifts were made in the earlier years of the building-programme and were undoubtedly intended to finance the cost involved by providing the additional revenues needed by the Abbey.

The site of the Church had already been consecrated by the Bishop in the presence of the founder and others; he marked out the area of the cemetery by placing four crosses to mark its boundary and then walked around it. The Church was planned in two sections – the eastern part where was placed the Lady Chapel and which was given absolute priority, and the western part containing the Nave for the use of the conversi which was deferred until the principal buildings around the cloister had been erected.

The erection of the Lady Chapel was an event of great importance. The laying of the first stone in the foundation was attended by the founder, the Bishop and the local clergy and laity. It was the Abbot or the Prior who laid the first stone and he probably placed five more in various places. A further six stones were laid by Monks which altogether totalled 12 stones placed in the form of a cross marking the outlines of the Church. The Bishop or his representative then dedicated the Church in the name of the Holy Trinity and the site of the Abbey to the honour of the Virgin Mary and All Saints, and condemned any person who should commit acts of violence within its boundary.

When the foundation was completed the next stage was the erection of the superstructure of the Lady Chapel and here another ceremony took place in the presence of a distinguished company. The Abbot and the community walked in procession from their temporary Chapel to the site singing psalms on the way. As they approached the place where the stone was to be laid they sung in antiphon, that is, by two groups of Monks singing and chanting alternately in a loud voice the *Gloria Patria*. The founder laid a corner-stone and probably two or there more each bearing the sign of the cross carved upon them while the choir sang *Te Deum* and *Salve Regina*. Other stones were laid by other distinguished persons and at the end of the ceremony the Abbot and the whole Convent on bended knees entreated the founder to accept the Lady Chapel as his place of burial, which he appears to have acceded to and gave the Abbot and brethren the privilege of carrying his remains to a place of interment before the High Altar. He was buried there on 24 November 1226, which indicates that the Lady Chapel was built by that date. In return for this privilege the founder gave the Abbey further land at Hawkerland near Collaton Raleigh.

The Sacristy in the south transept was the first part to be elevated and progress was then made on the North transept and then the Choir and Presbytery completed the Lady Chapel. It was roofed with lead and was rectangular in form, measuring about 70 ft long (21 m 5 dm) and about 35 ft in width (10 m 7 dm), with walls about six feet thick (2 m) on the north east and five feet thick (1m 5 dm) on the eastern side. Other walls varied between three feet and four feet thick (9 dm to 1 m 2 dm). Standing near the eastern wall in the Presbytery was the High Altar, an all-white edifice dedicated to the Holy Trinity and the Virgin Mary. In the transepts north and south were at least two altars or private Chapels in each and these were dedicated to Saints whose names have not come down to us. A most unusual feature was the extension of the eastern wall by an enclosed courtyard 10 ft (3 m 1 dm) in width with walls around it four feet (1 m 2 dm) in thickness. The only access to the courtyard was through a door in the wall at the south-west corner of the courtyard where it joined the south wall of the main structure. The only possible explanation of this unusual feature is that the enclosed courtyard was built to protect the eastern wall of the Lady Chapel from the floodwater of the Madford river which even today is liable to flooding. Without this protection the floodwater would have sapped away the foundations of the eastern wall and endangered the security of the High Altar and the burial place of the founder.

In the year 1225 the Abbey was visited by the Archbishop of Canterbury, Stephen Langton, and the Bishop of Exeter, William Brewer (nephew of the founder of the Abbey). It is most probable that they came to consecrate the Conventual Lady Chapel which was by this time erected. They were no doubt attended by the usual retinue of squires, valets, pages and servants and during their stay the Bishop issued a Charter relating to Hatherleigh which was dated from Dunkeswell 17 September 1225; included among the witnesses was the Archbishop of Canterbury, Stephen Langton. The visit of the two prelates of the Church to Dunkeswell at this time may also have been influenced by the presence of Lord William Brewer, the founder. This great man who, during his life-time, had played such an outstanding part in national and local life, had the previous year surrendered to the King all the land he held of the King and retired to the Abbey at Dunkeswell where he joined the Cistercian community as a lay brother. There is no doubt the two prelates were moved by a desire to meet again, possibly for the last time, the great man with whom both of them had been on terms of close friendship for many years. The following year Lord William Brewer died at the Abbey.

The foundations of the Lady Chapel almost in complete form were discovered in 1841, when the remains were cleared to provide for the erection of the present Holy Trinity Church upon part of the site of the Nave of the Conventual Church. Excavations then undertaken revealed remains of a 13th-century monumental pavement of coloured floor-tiles, and in the north-east corner of the Lady Chapel the remains of a tomb and monument which was

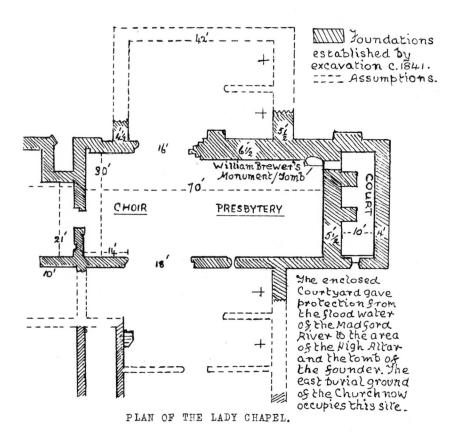

PLAN OF THE LADY CHAPEL.

undoubtedly that of the founder William Brewer. From the last remaining cor-belled face of a former Abbot which stands attached to the south-east corner of the remains of the gatehouse, we can most certainly conclude that the Lady Chapel contained many such images and niched figures upon its walls and arches. There was a stone tower above the crossing of the transepts which con-tained four bells. The Lady Chapel stood upon what is now the east burial ground of the present Church and on this spot for more than 300 years the professed brethren of the Abbey came regularly to fulfil their religious duties in song and prayer.

The provision of a water-supply and the laying down of a system of drainage was undertaken in the early stages of development. The area was well served by streams and springs of water and this was brought to the points of service through welded lead pipes while streams were walled in to pass running-water through tunnels to serve the foundations of the kitchen, rere dortors and other buildings, all of which were in a direct line of water flow south of the cloister. The running streams carried away all effluent to the Madford river which lay to the east. The Abbey Mill which was built later in the development was situated a short distance south of the claustral buildings and a diversion of water from the Madford river to provide the leat to work the mill most probably passed through the foundations of the claustral buildings on the south, on its way to rejoin the river. A stream approached the Abbey from the north west and this was used to feed two large fishponds which covered some two acres of land. The outflow of the two fishponds divided into two streams, one of which flowed along the northern boundary of the Abbey precinct and the other flowed south along the western frontage of the Abbey and then was diverted east to the river, serving on its way the claustral buildings of the south. The claustral buildings of the Abbey were surrounded on all sides by water and there was unlikely to have been any problem of pollution as the difference between pure and impure water was known. Water was purified by filtering it through beds of stone and sand and then taking it by lead pipe and conduit to serve personal and domestic and other uses wherever it was required. The Monasteries were in advance of their time in the matter of water-supplies and drainage-systems and were pioneers in this important field of social development. The precise evidence of the drainage-system, alas, lies below ground.

At this point in the building-programme there was a regular flow of flint and dressed stone, timber and metal, to the site, and its transport was by wagons drawn by oxen and horses over land tracks. The problem of transport in those early days was formidable and one would expect that the nearest sources of supply would be used. The main buildings were of flint stone with dressings of Beer Stone and Purbeck marble. The timber came mainly from the woodlands around the Abbey. The Cistercian Abbey at Cleeve, West Somerset, was under construction at the same time as the Abbey at Dunkeswell and as the Cistercians conformed to a general building-plan it is probable that both Abbeys had many features in common and obtained their building materials from the same source. As the Cistercian Abbeys of Forde and Newenham obtained supplies of stone from quarries at Whitestaunton it is very probable that Dunkeswell Abbey also did.

Around the Church the Abbey grew up and upon completion of the Lady Chapel the builders now directed their attention to the eastern range of the cloister. These buildings began with the Sacristy which was in fact a continua-

Cistercian Monks (*Monachi*)

Lay Brethren (*Conversi*), 1128–1348

tion of the south transept of the Lady Chapel, and was a chamber of small rectangular shape. It was the office of the Sacrist who was responsible for the fabric of the Church and its repair as well as for the shrines and the ornaments and vessels used in the Church services. Any treasure possessed by the Abbey was kept in safe custody in the Sacristy in which the sacrist himself slept at night to protect his charges and to be available to enter the Church at once if the occasion arose. His duties were many, including the supply of candles to the whole Convent and seeing that the many services in Church took place at the right times, and to ring the bell for them. He arranged the funeral obsequies for deceased brethren and he usually had an assistant Sub-Sacrist to help him; the assistant slept in the church at night.

Adjoining the sacristy southward was the Library with shelves and cupboards for books. This was in the care of the Precentor who was, among other things, the librarian, archivist and organiser of ceremonies and processions which took place from time to time. He arranged the services in church and instructed novices and young monks in music and the lessons. He kept a list of members of the community who died and had a key to the Abbey chest. He was the chief singer in the Abbey Choir and saw that all were present and understood the services.

The next chamber southward from the Library was the Chapter House, the

The passage-way south-east of the cloister as it must
have appeared

next place of importance after the Church. It was a chamber about 24 ft (7 m 4 dm) by 36 ft (11 m). Against the east wall was the Abbot's chair placed in the centre, while around the walls were stone benches for seating the brethren. In front of the Abbot's chair was the reading-desk and the centre of the chamber was open. At the end of Mass in Church – usually about 7.30 or 8 am each day – the great bell rang out for the daily chapter meeting.

The next chamber to the south of the Chapter House was the Parlour which was a small room and suitable for accommodating a few who wished to discuss matters of mutual interest. The Parlour in a later period contained a stairway leading to the dormitory above.

Then followed a passageway to the south-east of the precinct which marked the end of the eastern range. In the centre of this passage on the south side was a door leading into a large chamber known as the Calefactory or Warm Room, and which was part of the south range. The Warm Room was a large rectangular chamber where a fire was kept burning day and night from All Saints (November 1st) to Easter and was the only chamber where warmth was available to the brethren in winter, unless they were ill or under treatment in the Infirmary or doing duty in the kitchen. It was a common room to which the brethren were permitted to bring relatives and visitors and where they gathered in winter for general conversation after a stoup of wine or beer in the frater, or where they awaited the toll of the bell for Compline, the last service of the day. Feet-washing ceremonies also took place here and the floor was carpeted with straw.

The ground floor of the eastern range of buildings having been laid, the whole of it was now covered by a long and open chamber known as the dortor or dormitory and this had a massive roof of timber throughout the whole length of the range. It was thatched with reed or straw and in a later period tiled or slated. The walls were built with a series of lancet windows on each side and were unglazed but probably shuttered. The chamber was entirely open and without partitions except perhaps at the southern end, where it was usual to place a partition to divide the professed brethren from either the novices or the boys of the school who also slept there. In the south-east corner was a door and passage leading to the rere dortor near which, at night, a lantern was placed in a niche of the wall to light the way across.

Access to the dortor was from the stairs situated in the south-east corner of the cloister where the south range joined it. At the opposite end of the dortor where it joined the south transept of the Church was another flight of stairs, known as the night stairs, which connected the dortor with the Church. There was no form of heating in this large open chamber so that it was very cold in winter and it was lit at night by a specified number of candles placed in certain specified positions.

The professed slept here upon straw mattresses laid on the floor with their heads

Specimens of pavement found on the site of the old Conventual
Church at Dunkeswell Abbey, 1841

to the wall on each side so that there was a gangway between them. Down this gangway came the circator each night flashing his lantern to right and left to see if all were asleep and that the candles authorised by rule were in their right places for burning overnight. The floor was carpeted with straw.

The rere dortor situated at the south-east angle of the dortor was a long and narrow chamber with a row of seats placed near one of the walls. Over each seat was a window in the wall, each seat being partitioned off from the others. The chamber had an open timber roof thatched at first, but later was tiled or slated. Below the seat and underneath it flowed the walled up stream of water which carried away the effluent to the river. This drain or a diversion of it was designed also to pass through the foundation of the kitchen and the rere dortor of the conversi and on to provide the main drainage of the south side of the claustral buildings.

The Infirmary, which usually was situated in the south-east of the cloister, was most probably placed to the north-west of the precinct to avoid the flood water of the nearby Madford river. Among the group of buildings which stood to the north-west were some that closely resembled those necessary for such a use. The Infirmary was designed as a Hospital for the sick and a home for the aged and infirm members of the community, and stood detached from the main claustral buildings.

Having erected the Lady Chapel and the eastern range of buildings, the master mason and his craftsmen now turned their attention to the south range. The principal structure here was the Frater, an old English word for refectory or the place where meals were served and eaten. This was a large open chamber on the ground floor. It was carpeted with straw and originally had a thatched timbered roof. Situated in the western half of the south range, it was sited almost parallel with the Common or Warm Room but a gap was left between them and this was not bridged until a later period.

The Frater, used by the professed brethren, was a place of some importance to them as they regularly gathered here at certain times of the day. On the west of the Frater was the kitchen – a separate structure, but directly connected to the Frater to facilitate the moving of food through a hatch in the wall. The kitchen also served the Frater of the conversi from the opposite side of the kitchen. Access to the Frater of the professed was from the south-west of the cloister and near the entrance doorway, in a recess in the wall, was a trough of water for washing hands and face and a recess for towels, together with a stone for sharpening the knives used at meals. Inside the Frater the High Table was placed upon a raised platform parallel with the east wall and in the centre sat the Abbot with some of his officials around him. Any distinguished visitor staying for the meal sat at the Abbot's right hand. Other tables were placed parallel with the other walls, leaving a gap in the west wall for entry to the

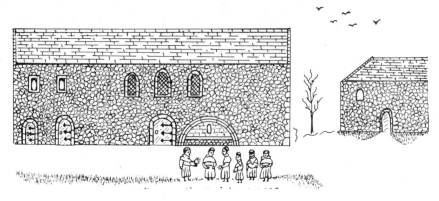

Dunkeswell Abbey: the *Frater* or south-cloister range as reconstructed from sketches made in 1794
and 1841

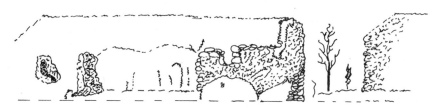

Dunkeswell Abbey: the ruins of the south-cloister range from a Simcoe sketch, c. 1841

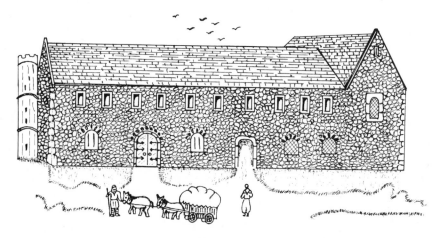

Dunkeswell Abbey: the west range reconstructed from known ruins and sketches of ruins made in
1794 and 1841. To the north the range adjoined the west frontage of the church

kitchen and access to the serving-hatch. Also standing about 88 ft or so above the floor was the pulpit which protruded into the Frater so that all could see it. This rectangular arrangement left an open space in the centre.

The kitchen was a free-standing structure from which the professed on the east side and the conversi on the west side could be served directly from the same centre as main meals took place at the same time. The kitchen was equipped with open fires above which were wide chimneys built into the walls and carried high above the roof. Over the fires were hung copper cauldrons to provide hot water for washing dishes and vessels and another for boiling vegetables, and one kept exclusively for the daily washing of hands, faces and heads and also for the feet-washing ceremonies which took place on Thursdays and Saturdays. Ovens were also heated from fires beneath them. The kitchen had a shute for disposing of kitchen waste and this undoubtedly went into the open drain stream which passed below the kitchen floor on its way to the river. There was also a handmill for grinding corn into flour, a well of pure water and a store for timber fuel to keep the fires burning. There was also a buttery and pantry. The cooks were appointed from the professed brethren at the Chapter meeting and they did this duty in weekly rotation, as also did the servers. The kitchen was always a busy place and fed at least 100 persons or more in its heyday. It was in the charge of the Kitchener, who was appointed by the Chapter, which drew up directions for his guidance. He was to see that noise in the kitchen was suppressed and to ask the sick daily what dish they relished and to supply it. He was to maintain supplies and keep the larderer supplied with meat (for the sick only), fish, fowls and other birds. He was to keep the accounts and report weekly to the Abbot. He was also enjoined to be careful what he did with the keys and not to trust the cooks too much, in view of the strong temptations before them. Badly cooked, stale or putrified foods must not be served and meals must be ready at the stipulated times. There must be close co-operation between the Kitchener and the Fraterer to see that the routine of the House was not disorganised and that meals therefore were cooked and ready at the right times. As there were no clocks and watches to check the time this was not as easy as it would seem. The kitchen was also served by a number of conversi in a subordinate position to the Kitchener and the cooks.

Having completed the south range the masons and craftsmen now turned their attention to the last stage of the first building-programme, that is, to the erection of the western range of buildings. Here on the western side of the cloister the conversi were established under the close supervision of the Cellarer, whose office and stores occupied a large part of this range. Between the cloister walk on the west and the western range itself was a small lane acting as an insulator of noise from the outer courtyard, so that the cloister could be kept as quiet as possible.

At the northern end of the west range was built on the ground floor a large chamber called a cellar or cellarium from which the monk in charge took the name of Cellarer – one of the most important offices in the community. The cellar was the storehouse and contained everything likely to be needed by the community, though in a later period additional storehouses were erected around the periphery of the outer courtyard. The cellarium was situated opposite the gatehouse through which all goods and supplies entered the outer courtyard, and it was therefore conveniently placed to receive the loads of corn, grain and other supplies brought to the House from the fields, gardens and granges as well as other supplies of materials, tools, timber etc. The additional storehouses that were later erected included a barn for storing rushes and straw used as floor-covering, a malthouse for brewing beer and a bakehouse and granary.

South of the Cellarer's stores on the ground floor was the Cellarer's office and a passage through the range into the cloister area. It was here that conversation took place between lay men and the brethren and especially between the Cellarer and the outsiders who supplied the community with goods and materials. It was here that the estates of the Abbey were controlled and directed and the labour of the conversi organised by the Cellarer.

The Frater of the conversi was the next chamber south of the Cellarer's office and passage. This was similar in all respects to the Frater of the professed except that at the High Table it was the Prior of the conversi who presided, but some time later it was the Cellarer who did this. Meals came from the same kitchen and the food was the same as that of the professed except that the bread allowance was larger and some helpings greater in recognition of the hard manual labour undertaken by the conversi.

The ground floor of the western range having been laid, the whole of it from north to south was roofed over with timber and thatched with reeds or straw – later to be replaced with slate or tiles. Beneath the roof was a long open chamber very much like the dortor of the professed in the east range. It was the dortor of the conversi. Lancet windows were set in the west wall and straw or rush mattresses placed on the floor to sleep upon. Here the conversi retired to sleep at about 8 pm and lay upon their straw mattresses upon the floor with their heads to the wall on each side, leaving a gangway between them in the centre. A little later the circator passed down the gangway with his lantern to see that all were accounted for and only approved candles left burning for the night. The conversi had similar religious duties to the professed but long hours of manual labour often some distance from the Abbey secured a variation in the services they attended. In recognition of this the conversi were exempted from the midnight service of Matins but they were aroused by their dortor bell at daybreak for the service of Prime, and in procession they went down their night stairs and into the Nave of the Church for the service. Until the Nave of the Conventual Church was built they used the temporary timber-built Chapel. When the service ended and under the direction of their Prior they went to their Frater for mixtum – breakfast – which consisted of half a pound of bread (454gr) and two thirds of a pint of beer (4dl) taken standing up, after which they proceeded to their daily tasks as directed by the Cellarer. At the south end of their dortor a passage led to their rere dortor.

The last link which completed the quadrangular group of buildings was the Nave of the Conventual Church, which when built joined up with the Lady Chapel to form the Abbey Church of St. Mary, within which the whole of the religious community could now worship but only in separate groups – the conversi in the Nave and the professed in the Lady Chapel. Between the two groups was a dividing-wall in the centre of which was a door about six feet wide which permitted access to both parts. It is believed that two rows each of six pillars supported the roof of the Nave and each side was aisled. The nave, as was the custom, was walled off from the aisles by stone screens erected between the pillars except for the west bays which were left open to provide passageways through the aisles. Against the stone screens were erected stalls for the conversi. The central area of the Nave, bounded by the walled screen on the north and south was the place allocated to the conversi for divine worship. In the north wall was a porch which led from the north aisle into the northern precinct, providing access to the cemetery and a means of entry into the Nave by lay persons, servants and guests lodged in the north-west of the Abbey precinct. The walls of the nave were about four feet thick (1 m 2 dm) and the roof was of lead. The nave altar stood a few feet westward of the dividing partition-wall and before it in the floor a marker was placed to indicate the spot upon which the Abbot stood on processional days, with the professed brethren standing behind him in two parallel rows in single-file stretching out towards the west door of the Nave. On each side of the procession stood the conversi and the lay people. For the whole community this was a great and solemn occasion in their cloistered lives.

How long it took the master mason and his craftsmen to complete the quadrangle of buildings around the cloister we do not know. There must have been a great deal of activity over a period of at least 25 years. The Lady Chapel and the nave of the Conventual Church were the most important of all the structures and were the most substantially built, having lead roofs. The remaining structures being of less importance would proportionately have been erected more quickly. Even so there were auxiliary buildings essential to the community, such as a stable for horses, a smithy, a carpenter's shop, a barn for the storage of hay, straw and rushes for carpeting the floors, a malthouse for brewing beer and a mill for grinding corn, a Guest House, and a number of

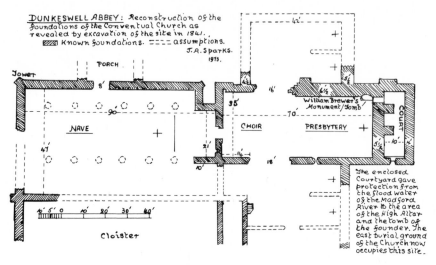

DUNKESWELL ABBEY: Reconstruction of the foundations of the Conventual Church as revealed by excavation of the site in 1841. [hatched] Known foundations. [dashed] assumptions.
J.A. Sparks.
1973.

PORCH

Tower

NAVE

CHOIR

PRESBYTERY

COURT

William Brewer's Monument/Tomb

The enclosed Courtyard gave protection from the flood water of the Madford River to the area of the High Altar and the tomb of the founder. The east burial ground of the Church now occupies this site.

Cloister

Reconstruction of the foundations of the Conventual Church

J.A.S.

The probable west frontage of the Conventual Church, from a Simcoe sketch, made in 1841, of the NW tower and adjoining wall with two windows

Thirteenth-century medallion windows from Simcoe sketches, c. 1840–41

other structures all necessary to the life of the Abbey. It seems clear that after the main structures had been erected some building continued on a smaller scale for years. By this time the home farm would have been brought into cultivation, and land around the Abbey used to grow crops, provide vegetable-gardens and fruit orchards. Some land comprised meadow and forest, pastures with herds of oxen, some sheep, swine and a few horses – all looked after by the conversi. Around the farm courtyard were the barns and other buildings needed for housing animals and storage. It is believed the Home Farm was established at nearby Stentwood and Bowerhayes.

Dunkeswell Abbey: the western gateway from known remains and Simcoe sketches, c. 1840.
Originally the roof would have been thatched

The western gatehouse (east frontage). Originally the roof would have been thatched

The mill was near at hand and also workshops used by the conversi and others who provided the skilled labour required for servicing the Abbey and its domestic establishment. Apple-orchards, fruit gardens, beehives, dovecotes and hawks for hunting game all helped to provision the Abbey. Hedges surrounded the fields of the Home Farm and these were often over-run by animals wandering into them from the common pasture nearby. Water was always available for domestic and farm use. Two large fish-ponds were constructed north-west of the precinct which provided a good supply of fish for the Convent tables. The Home Farm and the many activities associated with it provided the self-supporting basis for the domestic life of the Abbey, and this form of life was one that continued for centuries without any significant change.

The timbered porter's lodge had by now served its purpose and was replaced by the stone structure of the Gatehouse – an important outpost controlling access to the outer courtyard on its western boundary. Through this archway passed the carts, wagons and horsemen as well as individuals entering or leaving the Abbey precinct. In the early period the lodge-porter was a lay brother but later he was 'a wise old man whose ripeness of age will not permit

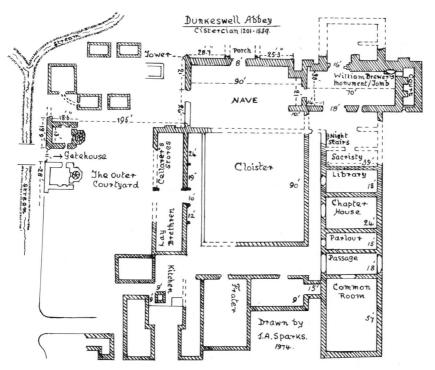

Plan of the Abbey

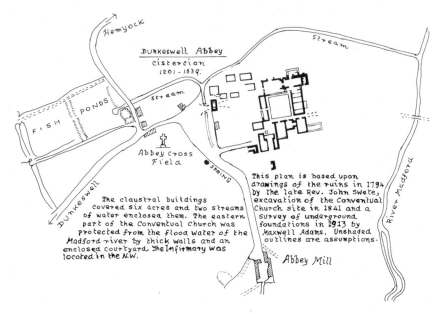

The Abbey and grounds

him to trifle' and he was a servant of the community. On each side of the archway on the ground floor was a chamber about 13 ft square (4 m), each containing a large fireplace, a window in the east wall and a doorway leading to a newel stairway giving access to a chamber above, which had a small window in its west wall which overlooking the approaches to the Gatehouse. This upper chamber had larger windows on its east side which overlooked the inner court-yard. The ground-floor chambers undoubtedly were used by the Gatehouse porter who was required to man the Gatehouse day and night and sleep there. Above the archway and the ground-floor chambers, and stretching the whole length of the Gatehouse, was a large chamber with windows in the west wall immediately above the arch which gave a commanding view of the approaches. Above this window on the external wall and just below the roof gable was a representation of the crucifixion. Covering the whole length of the Gatehouse was an open timbered and thatched roof which later was tiled. It seems clear that this large chamber, probably divided, was part of the Almonry which usually was established at or near the Gatehouse – the place where the poor and the sick came for alms and poor pilgrims and pensioners were housed.

The Guest House was a separate building not far from the Gatehouse. The temporary structure erected at the foundation was replaced by a permanent stone structure in the north-west precinct. Here came pilgrims and travellers seeking hospitality from the Abbey. In charge of the Guest House was the Hosteller, who was a person of some importance in an age when the monasteries provided the only accommodation available. The hospitality provided by the Abbey was free and of this full advantage was taken by many who could afford to pay. No one was turned away and any guest who was a stranger could stay two days and two nights without questioning as to his intentions.

We know from the registers of the Cistercian Abbey of Newenham that within five years of its foundation a school for boys existed in 1252 and that date was just two years after the first stone was laid in the building programme. This indicates the degree of priority with which the Cistercians regarded the formation of a school for boys: the Abbey at Dunkeswell would not have regarded it as less urgent. A separate school-building was provided outside the Gatehouse and most probably was placed where the present 'Old School House' now stands.

The cloister was the open centre around which were erected the buildings associated with the life of the community, and these were connected together by covered alleyways which provided a means of communication between them. In early days the four alleys were open on the cloister side and must have been very cold in winter, but later they were enclosed by ornamental stonework embracing glazed windows which improved the condition somewhat, although there was no form of heating. A lamp burned in each corner during hours of darkness.

CHAPTER TWO

Agriculture and the Estates

THE WHOLE of the superstructure described in the last chapter involved an outlay of substantial sums of money over many years, and the basis for providing it was the successful development of an agricultural economy on the land and estates of the Abbey. The acquisition of land by gift and purchase brought to the Abbey revenues with which to finance the building-programme and as that programme advanced the acquisition of land increased. Since the confirmation Charter of King John in 1206 substantial areas of land had been acquired and upon the death of the founder, Lord William Brewer, in 1226 the Abbot sought confirmation of the possessions of the Abbey from King Hery III – a very wise precaution as future Abbots at varying times were called upon by the Crown to prove entitlement to their possessions.

Henry III granted three confirmation Charters to the Abbey dated 4, 20 and 21 February 1227. The first confirmed the gift of William Brewer of the Manor of Hembury (Broadhembury) by far the largest of all its Manors. This Manor was held by William de Torynton who joined the Crusades to the Holy Land and gave the Manor to his Uncle Lord William Brewer who, in turn, gave it to the Abbey. According to the Doomsday Survey it comprised 480 acres of ploughland of which the Lord of the Manor ploughed 120 acres with two ploughs and 29 villeins ploughed 360 acres with ten ploughs. On the Manor were also 11 bordars, two swineherds who rendered to the Lord 10 swine yearly, six serfs, one packhorse, seven cattle, five swine, 100 sheep, a Mill tendering 50p yearly, 80 acres of woods, ten acres of meadow, 50 acres of pasture. It was worth £8 a year for taxation purposes.

The second Charter of Henry III confirmed the land held by the Abbey in 1206 and the following acquisitions since that date:

Land in the Manor of Uffculme with the Mill, the gift of William Brewer.

Bolham, Freschie, Bocland, Lodreford, Hickeresdon – all the land possessed there by the Abbey of Forde with all appurtenances and all their rights in Bywude.

Land at Linor (Leynor – S. W. Hackpen) and appurtenances, the concession of Robert, nephew of Robert le Goiz.

Hoked (Sheldon), all that land the gift of Amicia of Dun, namely that land Richard Cox and Senner his brother held.

The third Charter of Henry III confirmed yet another Charter of William Brewer and other acquisitions. The Charter gave land in return for the right of burial before the High Altar of the Conventual Church at Dunkeswell. This land was at Hawkerland in the Manor of Collaton Raleigh and comprised some 112 acres, of which 28 acres was the desmesne land of the Lord and 84 acres held by 11 peasants.

The following gifts were also confirmed in the Charters of Henry III:

Bridgewater: 'A messuage in the town of Bruges Walteri formerly held by William de Andresye, the gift of William Brewer'.

Escot: 'of the gift of Hugh de Hembiri', all his land of Escot, otherwise called Hoga, and all his rights therein'.

North of the Abbey: 'The gift of Richard de Hidon, land to the north of the Abbey, once held of him by Ralph the Baker, his servant, and all the land of Burgh (the Hill) viz: – four ferlings'. (30 acres).

Weringeston: (Buckerell): 'of the gift of William Oysun all his land of Weringeston'.

A substantial amount of land came into the possession of the Abbey after the 1227 confirmation Charters of Henry III. As far as the dates of acquisition are available they suggest substantial additions in the middle years of the 13th century, when the first building programme was near completion and the Abbey was able to turn its attention to the expansion and development of its growing estates. Much of this additional land came from gifts but there were some substantial purchases, which indicate that money was available and the mood of the Abbots expansionary.

The Manor of *Lincumbe* (Ilfracombe) was the last gift of land to the Abbey by the Founder, William Brewer, before he surrendered to the King all his lands in 1224. Abbot John in the Lincumbe Charter says William Brewer gave them this land 'for the upkeep of one candle burning night and day before the Greater Altar of the Monastery of Dunkeswelle beyond the tomb of the same William Brewer for the salvation of his soul'.

Some idea of the extent of the Manor of Lincumbe can be gathered from the Doomsday Survey, which says that the Manor included 240 acres of ploughland of which the Lord of the Manor had 60 acres and two ploughs. There were also eight villeins who ploughed 180 acres with five ploughs, nine

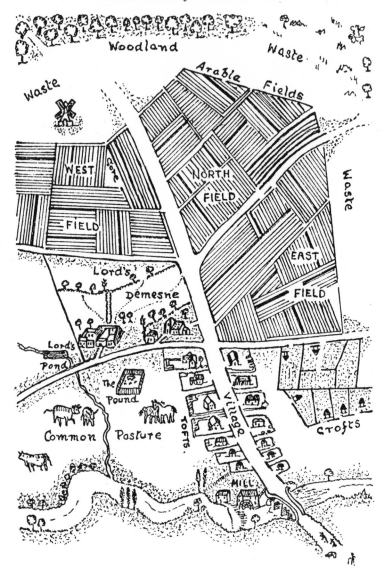

Plan of a Manor

bordars and three serfs, one packhorse, eight cattle, 12 swine, 100 sheep, 15 goats, 1½ acres of meadow and 100 acres of pasture, together worth yearly £3 for taxation purposes.

Buckland Brewer (5 miles S.W. of Bideford) 1233: In this year William Brewer, the son of the founder, died and the Abbey inherited a substantial estate subject to the provision that it was to revert to William Brewer should he

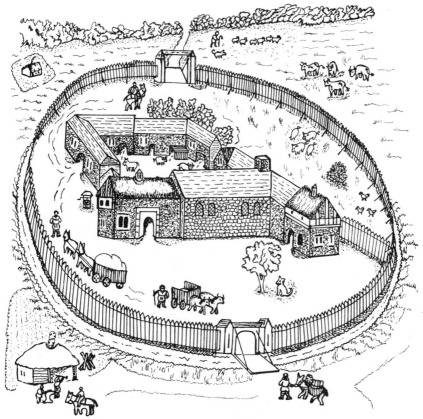

The house and hall of the Lord of the Manor, and the courtyard where the villagers sought refuge in times of violence (13th century)

have an heir born to him. As William died childless the Abbey was confirmed in its possession by a Charter given to it by the son of the founder which also provided that the Abbey should have the right to go to the Hundred Court of 'Brokeland' for the recovery of its rights and claims.

The Manor of Coleton (Collaton Raleigh): 1228 at Exeter on 25 July the Abbot purchased from Richard de Crues 368 acres of land for 5 marks of silver (£3.33p).

The Manor of Weringeston (Buckerell) 1253: On 13 October Thomas de Cyrencestre and Avice his wife granted to the Abbey 105 acres of land in Weringeston in free alms for ever. The Abbey to pay scutage of £2 (a tax on land in lieu of military service), and for all services upon the land when it shall fall due, suit of Court (the right to go to the Hundred Court for the recovery of rights and claims), customs and exactions. The Abbot gave Thomas and Avice £5.

Dining in the Manor Hall where the Lord provided liberal and free hospitality for all classes. The upper class at the top table were served wine, roast venison and pork, game and poultry stuffed with herbs, and fish served with sauce. At the lower table ale was drunk, and boiled mutton and beef served, eaten with thick hunks of bread. Straw was spread over the floor and dogs were always present. Frequently, though not always, a musician played during the meal

Ploughing and sowing (Lutterell Psalter, 1340)

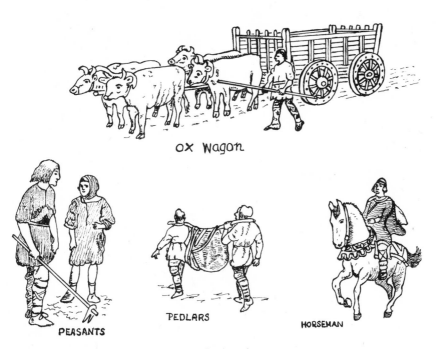

ox wagon

PEASANTS PEDLARS HORSEMAN

Medieval people

Broadhembury, mid-13th century: Geoffrey Coffin, Kt., and Juneta his wife gave the Abbey 'all his land at Buvi . . . saving to his men of Lyveton and Puttynheghes free passage with their animals by the highway from Lyveton to the hill of Hembyr' to their feedings, so that his men may not be troubled by the Monks on account of their animals passing by the highway, unless the animals be found in the said tenement with a watch set . . .' (Wriothesley Deed 45 Hampshire R.O.)

Broadhembury 2 April 1251: William de Botelerehegh gave all his land lying next to the land of the Monks in the furlong of Mapeldurelonde in exchange for a similar furlong of Abbey land called Bremilond.

29 September 1253: By Indenture between the Prior and Brethren of St. John of Jerusalem and the Abbey, the Prior resigns the Mill and land at Broadhembury including 80 acres of arable land at Ruffgreihay for an annual payment of £1.25p.

About the same time the Prior and Brethren of the Order of St. John of Jerusalem resigned to the Abbey three ferlings of land at Catecombe and about 137 acres of moor and waste at Combhangerwood (three parts of the wood and situated between Broadhembury and Sheldon) for which the Abbey agreed to make an annual payment of 50p. This Order had a small Priory at nearby Bodmescombe.

18 November 1255: Peter le Bon and Alienora his wife gave the Abbey one ferling of land in Ruffgreihays and the Abbot received them into all the benefits and orisons which hereafter shall be done in his Church of Dunkeswell for ever.

25 November 1256: John de Gendeford and Nichola, his wife, gave the Abbey one messuage and one ploughland in Hembury for which the Abbot received them into all benefits and orisons which henceforth shall be done in his Church for ever.

12 March 1260: In return for two pieces of land lying north and west of the Abbey Grange at Broadhembury consisting of about eight acres, Abbot John granted Canon Martin and the Church at Broadhembury a meadow near the Church lying between the Abbey Grange and the village, and a piece of land about seven acres near the yard of the Church 'saving to the Abbey the water course to their Mill of Hembyr' and the cleansing of the bed of the same water as often as need be'.

Mid-13th century: Roger Evered gave the Abbey his land at Bosewode (Broadhembury) for which the Abbot gave him 20 marks (£13.33p) in recognition.

11 July 1373: Chaplains Robert Pencrych, Alexander Tympayn, John Wellisford and John Bitlesgate gave the Abbey: 'all their messuages, lands and tenements and the rents and services of all their tenants, as well free as villein, in Lyveton and Puttynheghe' (Broadhembury).

To find a torch to burn continually before the High Altar in honour of the body of Christ in the Abbey Church of St. Mary. The Abbey also had to pay £5 to the King for his license to receive it. The land comprised about 116 acres and 60p rent. (Hampshire R.O. Wriothesley Deeds 50/54, 109).

Upottery: A tenement which brought in a rent of 20p in 1291.

Sainthill, Kentisbeare Parish: Land and appurtenances the date of acquisition being unknown.

Cheriton Phippeyn: A tenement paying a rent of 25p. Date of acquisition unknown.

Exeter: A messuage in the Parish of St. Paul's. Date of acquisition unknown. It was most likely the Abbot's town house and where he resided on occasions when his presence was necessary in connection with ecclesiastical affairs in the Diocese.

Honiton: A tenement and garden in 'Burgo de Honyton' lying and being near to the estate of Catherine Carew's heirs on the west and the estate of the heirs of Wm. Courtenay called Le Place on the east. Date of acquisition unknown. It was most likely used in connection with the administration of the Abbey estates to the west and south of Honiton.

Repalyngheys: Land between Giddesham and Honiton including the whole of the Giddesham Mount. The source of acquisition of this land is unknown but it was probably acquired in the 14th century and was a substantial area of land let on 4 October 1525 on lease to Agnes Vowler, widow, and her sons Christopher and George and lately occupied by her husband Nicholas. Leased for their several lives for an annual rent of £3.17p.

12 May 1458: A large area of land known as Madford, Madeshamel, and Gorwell was let by the King to the Abbey for ten years for a yearly rent of £4.33p with a proviso for an increase. This land was escheated to the King upon the death in 1399 of the Lord of the Manor of Hemyock, Sir William Asthorpe, he being a bastard and without heir. The land adjoined the Abbey precinct on the eastern side of the Madford river.

This accounts for all the known sources of the land possessions of Dunkeswell Abbey, which could not have been far short of some 10,000 acres. There is no trace of any sales of land although there were a few small exchanges before 1285, but after this date a religious House could not alienate land given to it under pain of forfeiture to the donors or their heirs. It follows that the land remained in the possession of the Abbey for some 300 years.

The Cistercians were essentially an agricultural community and they had ideas of their own as to how the land should be cultivated. The Manorial system of cultivation established upon the extensive estates that they had acquired was not their way of doing things. They were confronted with an arable system of cultivation based upon three large open fields divided into

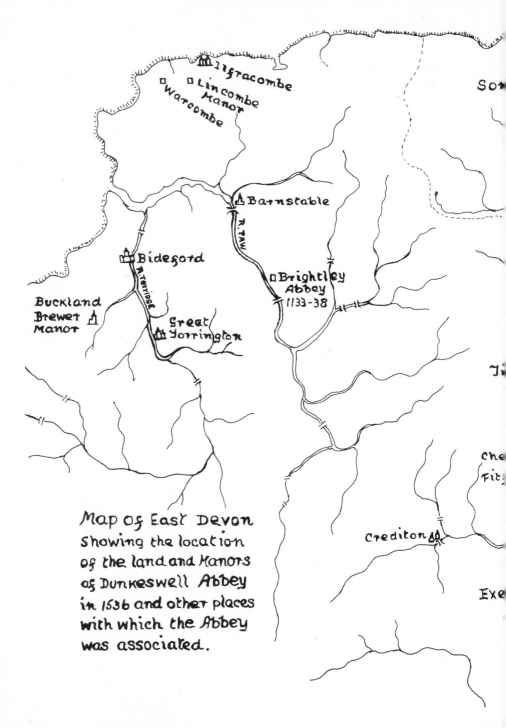

Map of East Devon
showing the location
of the land and Manors
of Dunkeswell Abbey
in 1536 and other places
with which the Abbey
was associated.

et

Cleeve
Abbey

Somerset

Wellington (Som)
Uffculme
Craddock
Culmstock
Hemyock
Clayhidon

Canons
Leigh
Abbey

BLACKDOWN

Whitestanton (Som)

on

Bolham
Man.

R. EXE

Hackpen
Manor

Dunkeswell
Abbey

Sheldon
Manor

Bowerhayes Manor

Forde
Abbey

Dunkeswell

Cullompton

Wolford

Shabcombe Manor

Broadhembury
Manor

Axminster

Payhembury

R. CULME

Wolveston manor

Weryngston
Buckerell

man.

Honiton

Newenham
Abbey

Dorset

e

Hill of
Gittisham
Rapplyngisheys
Manot

R. AXE

Ottery
St. Mary

Hawkerland
Manor

Clyst

Dotton
Manor

R. EXE

Collaton
Raleigh
Manor

R. OTTER

Map of East Devon

Typical thirteenth-century village

many separate strips of land each about one acre in extent and each strip cultivated by a different individual. The individual in turn had other strips of land spread over the fields in different locations, the total acreage of which could be anything up to 30 acres. These open fields belonged to the Lord of the Manor and one field of the three lay fallow each year. The Cistercian objective was to consolidate these strips of land into large areas, enclose them and cultivate them under their own direction and control. Likewise with the meadow-land which was similarly marked out into individual strips, they proposed to unify this into large areas, cut the grass and harvest the hay for their own use. The open areas of pasture-land they sought to use for feeding large flocks and herds of cattle and sheep. This involved the disappearance of the villeins, bordars and serfs and the growth of a free wage labouring force who would work for wages under the direction of the Cistercians. These were times, however, when custom was the law and the customs entrenched in manorial society were far from easy to put aside. The centre of economic life was the Manor and this was based upon the rights of individuals to the use of the land within its jurisdiction; thus the changes proposed by the Cistercians would undermine those rights and the authority of the Manor. The Cistercians, however, made steady progress as their way of doing things proved more economical and brought substantial improvements to agriculture, and in due time this was recognised. In the meantime the Abbots found themselves Lords of Manors having to administer the old order based upon custom while at the same time seeking to make the changes they desired. This presented them with formidable problems and great hostility from local people threatened with dispossession of their ancient rights in the land, and customs that had been entrenched for centuries of time. The people resided in a village on the Manor usually at a centre point where roads crossed a stream. Fifty to sixty people made up a large village. Near the centre was the Church and the Manor Hall. Along the tracks stretching out from the centre were the dwellings of the community, each enclosed by a hedge. With the exception of a few free tenants the people were tied to the Manor and could not leave it. The villeins, by far the largest number, held their strips of land in the open fields from the Lord who also supplied each villein, when he first took up his holding, with one cow, two oxen, six sheep together with some tools and household utensils, and the villein had the right to feed his livestock on the common pasture and wasteland of the Manor. In return for this the villein laboured on the Lord's desmesne land for a period of time which depended upon the extent of his land-holding, which could be anything up to 30 acres. The Cistercian agricultural objectives undermined this way of life and changed the basis of society.

The Cistercians first started with the land that had been given to them and took every opportunity when strips of land fell vacant through death or other causes to combine individual strips into larger units, and to this they added where they could purchases of adjoining land. Another method, most successfully pursued throughout the 13th century, was the clearance of moor and wasteland of scrub and undergrowth and ploughing it up, draining marshes and clearing forests to provide more ploughland, meadow and pasture. By this method the complications of the open-field strip system were by-passed as new land brought into cultivation in this way by the Lord of the Manor (the Abbot) could be formed into large fields limited only by the extent of the assarting operations. It involved considerable effort sustained over long periods of time and until about 1277 it was done mainly by the conversi and the professed monks working together with what free labour they could find. After the year 1277 the professed withdrew from assarting operations and the conversi were left to spearhead these operations with whatever labour could be got to help them. It became the policy of the Abbey at this time to grant charters to free tenants and to make it a condition of their tenure that they assist the assarting operations of the Abbey at certain times of the year.

An interesting Charter granted by Abbot Ralph during his Abbacy in the years 1249–51 indicates the conditions at that time which were attached to free tenancies. The essential part of the Charter taken from a 16th-century translation of the original 13th-century text is as follows:

To all the faithful in Christ this present writing seeing and hearing: Father Ralph, Lord Abbot of Dunkeswell (1249–51) and the Convent of the same place greeting in the Eternal God:

Know all of you that we have delivered over and granted to Walter de la Hego the brother of Richard de la Hego and to the heirs of his body lawfully begotten that ground which Richard sometime Vicar of Sheldon for 10p yearly sometime held of us and is contained within the bounds following: [Then follows a description of the boundaries of the land which seem to be contained within a series of ditches], . . . to have and to hold the said lands with appurtenances to him and the heirs of his body to be begotten of us and our successors free, quietly, peacably and entirely for ever rendering therefore yearly to us and our successors he and his heirs 15p sterling at three terms in the year towitt at Easter, on the Nativity of St. John the Baptist (June 24th) and the Feast of St. Margaret (November 16th) by equal portions and in the Purification of the Blessed Mary (February 2nd) one pound (454 gr) of wax or sixpence (2½p) at their pleasure for all services and demands saving Royal service such as belongs to the said tenement, saving also this that the said Walter and his heirs to us and our successors in winter our Downe either to (assart) as we shall choose or to plow and in the Autumn tryst with us to mowe and our Court of Sheldon fully to follow shall be held (The Manor Court to arrange).

We moreover grant to the said Walter and his heirs that which our villeins turbary and common of pasture they may not Soe, that of our waste as us it shall please our profit always we may make. We grant therefore that they and their posterity be free from us from all villeinage but this land with its appurtenances and with all the covenant aforesaid we and our successors warrant the said Walter and the heirs of his body begotten against all men and we are bound to warrant. (East Devon R.O. D12/21/1).

This Charter was granted at a time when the Abbey was in the early stages of developing an agricultural community at Sheldon. It had quite recently received the Church at Sheldon and its lands from the Bishop and was acquiring extensive areas of woodland, down and wasteland in the locality. There is no doubt that this Charter was one of a number granted by the Abbots at this time as more and more wasteland was being reclaimed for cultivation and free tenants were being sought to assist in the effort. It is doubtful if the villein could have been commanded to take part in assarting operations, as his status was already determined by the custom of the Manor in which he already held land in the open fields and meadows, but there is no doubt that some were encouraged to take up free tenancies at a nominal rent on condition that they assisted the Abbey in its assarting operations. Some bordars and cottars too found exemption from their servile status attractive when it was coupled with regular wage-payments by the Abbey in return for their labour.

The unflagging efforts of the Abbey at Sheldon produced a significant increase in the cultivated land of the Parish and resulted in a flourishing Manor, with its Grange farm, messuages and tenements producing a regular rotation of crops and an increasing number of cattle, sheep and other livestock and a regular and increasing revenue. What they accomplished at Sheldon they also achieved in greater or lesser degree in the remaining Manors on their estates.

When the unit of land brought together reached some 200/300 acres a Grange farm was formed. A group of buildings were erected and these were enclosed by a wall or ditch and within this enclosure was built a granary for storing the corn at harvest and a barn if it was an arable Grange, or, if it was a livestock Grange then the buildings were cattle byres, stables and storage for winter feeding of cattle, sheep, pigs or whatever form of livestock was kept. If the Grange was some distance away from the Abbey a Domus Principalem was also built; that is, a dwelling incorporating a dormitory, refectory and a common or warm room as well as a Chapel for the use of the conversi and any others associated with the life of the Grange. These Granges were cells of the Abbey where the conversi resided for a period and then returned to the Abbey and others took their place. The land of the Grange was enclosed by ditches and banked up earth, a hedge or wall or a natural boundary, and could be a combination of all of these, the idea being to isolate the Grange and prevent outside encroachment upon its territory. The development of Granges and large-scale farming units received great benefit from the regular exchange of information between the Cistercian Houses as knowledge of improvements and development was passed on from House to House by visiting Monks. The importance of fertilisers to improve the yield of crops was increasingly appreciated and the spreading of manure over the fields from a growing number of farm animals became a systematic activity in the process of cultivation. Ploughing in the arable fields in the early period was done by oxen – eight oxen constituted a plough team which was considered capable of ploughing about 120 acres called a carucate. The carucate was divided into eight bovates – one bovate (one ox) was equal to about 15 acres and two bovates equalled about 30 acres which was called a virgate. Therefore four virgates or eight bovates constituted one carucate which was also known as a hide. The decision whether to establish a Grange and whether it should be arable, livestock or a mixed farming Grange was a decision taken in the Chapter House of the professed Monks, and they made any subsequent decisions which arose from the new order they were carving out of the old agricultural system that absorbed a major part of their time and activity.

In the process of developing the Granges local people were often displaced and they had to be re-settled in other parts, but this was not always undertaken as the records of the Bishop of Exeter show. When the Parish Church of Doddeton (Dotton, Collaton Raleigh) with all its land was given to the Abbey by Bishop William Brewer, nephew of the founder, on 30 September 1242, the Abbot and Convent took possession of the land and compelled the cultivators to move away. They closed the Church and took away the baptismal font and the bells and most probably used the Church as the centre from which to organise the cultivation of the land of the Parish in the form of a Grange. Some 17 years later, Bishop Walter Bronescombe visited the Parish and when he discovered what had happened his reaction may best be described from the record in his Register dated 5 February 1259:

Walter, Bishop of Exeter, both a former parishioner of the Church of St. David of Doddeton and still cherished as a son by the beloved lay inhabitants of the parish, which Bishop William is said to have brought together and granted for the special uses of our predecessors, having visited the parish as in duty bound, discovered that the Monks had ejected the parishioners, prevented them from farming the land, and cut them off from the divine estate of the Church which they have profaned. We have therefore ordered the Monks themselves to come forward and answer the charges.

When the Abbot and Monks appeared before us and were asked whether they wished to answer the charges made against them, they finally answered that they wished to obey our commands and that they supported our consecration and promised to observe it and never wilfully to attack it.

Since therefore we consider it imperative to preserve the Church at Doddeton, to provide for the safety of our souls and the general good we declare it our wish to observe the canons of our predecessors and desire them to be kept by our successors. We have therefore decreed with the advice and assent of our beloved sons, the deacons and members of the Chapter of Exeter that the Church itself and all its possessions should be restored and so preserved under a debt of honesty; that divine service should be celebrated either by the monks themselves or by secular presbyters as it was before, and that all lands, rights and privileges should be restored. In addition we decree that if the monks attempt not to observe this our consecration, then whatever rights they may be said to have in the said Church shall be alienated. In which matter let this be a testimony. Given at Exeter on the feast of St. Agatha Virgin (5 February 1259) and the second year of our consecration.

The Church remained in the possession of the Abbey for 297 years until the dissolution in 1539 but it was then known as the Church of St. Mary at Dotton. The monks kept their promise to Bishop Bronescombe and maintained the Parish Church there to the end.

The policy of consolidating land into larger units continued but the Grange system had its limits. It was found difficult to control the administration of the Grange if it was situated too far away from the Abbey precinct and the conversi, upon whom the Abbey relied to work and manage the Grange farms, were now a disappearing quantity as the sources of new recruits to their ranks withered away and finally dried up. The Cistercians therefore had to rely more upon the employment of bailiffs to manage their Granges but they continued nevertheless to consolidate their lands into larger units and to develop the system of tenant farming. The farm units which they created consisted of an area enclosed by a stone wall within which was built a family dwelling (farmhouse), farm buildings and a garden; allocated to it was land which varied in acreage. This land could be arable for corn-growing, pasture and meadow for livestock or a combination of both. These farms were known as messuages and often were leased for life to tenants and their wives and children and provided with livestock and equipment. The tenants of the larger farms were free of labour obligations to the Abbey, for the rents they paid for their leases took account of this. When the tenant died a 'heriot' was usually paid to the Abbey in the form of the best beast or its value and this was an acknowledgement of the livestock and equipment provided by the Abbey with the land and which in theory should be returned to the Abbey when the tenant to whom it was originally loaned died. The payment of the heriot ensured that the livestock and equipment remained for the use of the succeeding tenant who was usually another member of the family. The 'heriot' system was also an acknowledgement that the land originally carried with it an obligation of labour service for the Lord of the Manor.

Smaller holdings of land were also organised and called tenements, which consisted of a dwelling and garden only which was enclosed by a wall or hedge. Some land was allocated to some tenements which varied in quantity and of these tenants some were free of labour service to the Abbey and some were not, depending upon the conditions attached to their tenements. Those who were free paid more rent for their tenements but they were free to spend all their time upon their land if it was large enough, or if it not, they could offer their labour for wages to the Abbey Grange or to the farmers of large holdings. Those tenants who were not free usually paid less rent for their tenements but were obliged to perform free labour service for the Abbey for verying periods of time according to the conditions of their tenancy. The obligation to labour for the Lord of the Manor (the Abbey) was not now determined by whether the tenant was a villein, bordar or cottar but by the conditions attached to the land which they held, and even this obligation was steadily being commuted to a money payment added to the rent. The holders of small tenements were increasingly forming themselves into free wage-labouring groups who secured their livelihood as farm-workers, carpenters, blacksmiths, and rural craftsmen, all of whom were essential elements in the new agricultural system. A sample of two leases granted by Abbot Ley for tenements in Lyvton, Broadhembury indicate how servile labour attached to the land of a tenement was commuted for money payment:

3rd May 1532: To Thomas Salter of Broadhembury and two others, the reversion of a cottage there for their several lives. Rent 40p yearly and £1 at Michaelmas (29th September) in lieu of labour for the Abbot in the Autumn.

30th September 1532: To Jane and Thomas Lane for three lives. Rent of two tenements and some other property £1.60p yearly and also 6p instead of 15 days labour for the Abbot in the Autumn, besides 1p at Michaelmas.

Spinning   Weaving

In most households wool and flax were spun into thread which was woven into cloth for clothing and other domestic fabrics – essentially a woman's occupation. Those who spun were known as 'spinsters' – a description that has come down to our own day to describe unmarried women.

The fundamental changes made by the Cistercians in agriculture by the creation of their Grange farms and the encouragement given to free tenancies of consolidated land-holdings laid the foundation of the individual farming system which has come down to our own times. The individual farmer now stood or fell by his own ability to organise profitably the cultivation of his landholding, most if not all of which was located around his farm homestead instead of being scattered in smaller pieces over a wide area. Also a source of free labour was opening up which allowed him to employ wage labour to assist him in his effort. The open-field strip system of the Manor, although seriously undermined by the new development, did not completely disappear and even as late as the dissolution of the monasteries in 1539 the Manor Courts were functioning and

Fourteenth-century housewife; storing water; a tethered hen (Lutterell Psalter)

collecting the rents for the Lord and levying fines upon those who failed to maintain the code of the Manor in relation to land-use. The new system, however, set the pace for agriculture which in turn largely created the basis for the growth of towns and the crafts by providing a growing and more regular supply of the products of the land for individual consumption by town-dwellers. The growth of the towns and of the crafts in turn created an increasing demand for the products of agriculture. To serve the demands of this increasing two-way traffic improved and expanding marketing arrangements developed. In the vanguard of this movement were the Granges directly farmed by the Abbey through a system of Stewards and Bailiffs. They were models of agricultural management in those times, and behind them came the free tenant-farmers with holdings of up to 100 acres, whereas the villeins, bordars, cottars and serfs with their open-field strips and servile labour were a declining element in Manorial life.

By the year 1291 the Abbey and its estates were well established, and we learn from page 152 of the 'Taxation of Pope Nicholas IV' that the income received by Dunkeswell Abbey from its possessions were:

The Abbot of Dunkeswell received from the	
Manor of Wulferchurche (Wolford)	£5.80p
Biwode (Dunkeswell)	3.30p
Burhei and Steintewode (Dunkeswell)	4.30p
Auliscombe	2.40p
Dunkeswell	2.20p
Sheldon	4.20p
Hidon (Clayhidon)	1.50p
Loveputt (Luppitt)	1.83p
Epotery (Upottery)	20p
Manor of Hemburi (Broadhembury)	10.00p
Huggeton (Payhembury)	80p
Weringeston (Buckerell)	1.50p
Sengetil (Sainthill)	15p
Hawkerlond (Near Ailsbeare)	3.70p
Dodeton (near Collaton Raleigh)	1.47p
Manor of Hankepenne (Hackpen, Uffculme)	7.17p
Manor of Boclande Bruer (Buckland Brewer)	7.40p
Manor of Lincumbe (near Ilfracombe)	6.68p
	£64.60p

The Abbot received from Spiritual sources	
the following revenue:	
The Church of Auliscombe (Rectory)	10.00p
The Church of Sheldon	3.35p
The Church of Dunkeswell	5.00p
The Church of Dotton	67p
	£83.62p

This statement was compiled by the Abbot as the basis of assessment for the tax of one tenth on ecclesiastical property to provide a subsidy granted for six years by the Pope to King Edward I to meet expenses of the expedition he was sending to the Holy Land in the Crusades. It was designed to provide a correct valuation upon which all future taxes of one tenth or one fifteenth could be based and it remained the basis until 1535. The tax paid by the Abbey upon the above assessment at the rate of one tenth was £8.36p. To appreciate those figures in their proper perspective it is necessary to consider them in relation to 13th–14th-century prices.

The price of a sheep weighing on average 18.16 kg (40 lb.) was about 5p to 10p. The fleece of wool upon that sheep on average weighed 674 g (1 lb 7¾ oz.) and was worth 3p or about half the value of the sheep.

An ox weighing 181–5 kg (400 lb.) was worth 55p and 10p for its hide, while the meat was priced at 00–2p for 454 gr. (½d a lb). A cow was worth 47p and a fowl 0·4p (1d).

A horse (saddle or cart) was worth 63p to 70p and a mare a little more.

The rent of arable land let to tenants was about 2½p an acre and to buy an acre could cost about 20p to 30p. Large acreages seem to have been sold for far less. For instance the Abbot bought 368 acres of land in Collaton Manor for 5 marks of silver which is equivalent to less than 1p an acre. In 1253 at Weringeston (Buckerell) the Abbot bought 105 acres of land for £5 which is less than 5p (11.4d) an acre.

Rent of a cottage tenement was 6p to 10p a year plus some days' labour for the Abbey at hay and corn harvest.

Omitting exceptional rates paid for piece work, the wages of an agricultural labourer would be at a rate of £2.58p yearly (or about 5p a week) ... When one finds day work, pay for it is about the rate of less than 1p (2d) a day for men, 0·4p (1d) for women and 0·2p (½d) a day for a boy. (Thorold Rogers: *Six Centuries of work and wages*)

The farm-servant as distinct from the labourer, and applying mostly to single men who received board at certain periods, aggregated to about £1.78p for a year's service (or 3½d a week).

The cost of reaping a crop of wheat, beans, peas, vetches or mowing grass for hay was about 2p (5d) an acre.

CHAPTER THREE

Temporal Responsibilities

Temporal Responsibilities: Manor life under Abbey jurisdiction. Boundary conflicts – violence in Hackpen Manor. Disputes with the Hospitallers of Bodmescombe. Common pasture on Hembury Downe. The Abbot as keeper of the King's Peace.

THE LIFE of an Abbey was based upon two main fields of activity, namely, the temporal and the spiritual. In the early period the temporal responsibilities overshadowed the spiritual and made heavy demands upon the time and attention of all members of the community. With the large areas of land which came into their possession there came also a large number of people who were attached to the land and obtained their livelihood from its cultivation. Their activities were regulated by the Manor Courts over which the Abbot or his representative presided and gave judgement. The people who resided in the Manor were formed into groups according to Feudal tradition. Each Manor had a small number of free tenants who paid a money rent for the land they occupied and were free of labour service on the Lord's demesne and free to move elsewhere. The much larger group of 'villeins' were tied for life to the Manor and gave specified periods of labour service to the Lord in return for the use of a dwelling-house and strips of land for cultivation. Each held up to 30 acres of land in strips scattered over three or more open fields. There were smaller groups of 'bordars and cottars' who occupied a dwelling and a small area of land, perhaps about an acre. These groups, not so fully occupied in cultivating the land, fulfilled the need of every Manor for blacksmiths, carpenters and craftsmen, and they contributed a measure of labour service for the Lord in return for their use of a dwelling and an acre or so of land. They also, as time went on, became a source of free wage labour useful to the free tenant, the villein or the Lord as they required assistance. The co-ordination of these groups within the Manor unit, the allocation among them of cattle, sheep and other animals all of which was regulated in minute detail by the Manor Court, called for the closest attention by the Abbot and his Chapter to the day-to-day activity upon their widespread estates.

While accepting their responsibility to the Manorial system which they inherited with their land, they nevertheless used those Courts to consolidate strip-land into larger units and to develop Grange farms comprising some 200/300 acres wherever they could. In addition, in most of their Manors the Abbots had jurisdiction over the behaviour and conduct of the people living on their Manors including the infliction of capital punishment by hanging for theft and felony. The Abbots also determined the price and quality of bread, ale and corn. These widespread civic responsibilities overshadowed the spiritual duties of the Cistercians in the early period when every monk, be he lay or professed, had some share in the temporal activities of the Abbey. Not the least among their temporal problems were the absence of clearly defined boundaries which were a continual source of friction over a long period of time, sometimes involving violence between adjoining Manors and owners of land. The Manor cattle and animals wandered over the common open pasture which had no bounds beyond a stream, a ditch or a fringe of trees. The landscape around as far as the eye could see was one vast open space of moor and woodland criss-crossed by animal tracks. The woodlands and the impenetrable forests were taboo to ordinary folk whose fear of demons and wild animals placed limits upon the extent to which they entered them. As Manors grew and extended their land areas over uncharted landscapes, disputes frequently arose as to where the boundary of one Manor ended and the boundary of another began. Against this background the Crown was frequently called upon to define the boundaries, and to this end the Sheriff of Devon was frequently directed by the Crown to proceed with 12 'wise and lawful men' to the scene of the dispute and there to determine the boundaries.

The Abbey had large areas of land in the Manor of Uffculme and frequently over many years disputes arose with the Lord of the Manor of Uffculme as to boundaries and rights of pasture.

Medieval surgery: extracting an arrow, and a head operation

The first we hear of the Abbey's presence in Uffculme was around the year 1210, when the Abbot diverted the course of water 'to the hurt of the free tenement of William Painel'. He was ordered by a Jury of the Assize Court to restore the course of the water and was fined for having diverted it.

Constant conflicts continued with the Lord of the Manor of Uffculme, and on his death around the year 1249 the Abbey sought an agreement with his successor John de Bolun and Alda his wife, regulating the rights of each in the Manor. The agreement reached, dated 1 July 1249 at Ilchester, defined the land upon which each party had rights of common pasture. It recognised the right of the Lord of the Manor to common pasture in the lands, woods, meadows and pasture in the Township of Uffculme but gave the Abbey these rights on the Hill called Hackpen for all their cattle of Hackpen, Craddock, Northcote, Slade, Hylle, Wombrook, Ashill, Suthewell, Smythencote, Hegh and Goodleigh. The agreement in fact established the Manor of Hackpen with its Court located at Craddock.

A dispute of a more serious character broke out on 28 December 1299 when John Cogan, the Lord of the Manor of Uffculme, his son Thomas, Philip of Cogan with 15 others broke into the Manor of Hackpen and drove out the monks and conversi whom they found there, assaulted and wounded two servants of the Abbey, damaged the Manor House, pulled down the gallows they found there and carried it off to Uffculme and burned it. In addition they stole about 60 oxen and 20 cows and drove them to Uffculme where they killed three oxen and wounded others. Altogether the Abbot declared that the Abbey suffered £100 worth of damage.

A trial took place before a Jury of 12 men. They confirmed the assault and assessed damages at £80, but found that it had not been done by the order and consent of John Cogan, the Lord of the Manor of Uffculme, who nevertheless had commanded and assented to the destruction of the gallows which he considered prejudiced his own liberties in his adjoining Manor where he too had the right to erect gallows and apprehend thieves. However, when once the thing had been done he sheltered them, he said, and continued to shelter many of them in his household.

A descendant of John Cogan, Sir William Cogan, Knight, in the year 1378 on September 22nd took action against the Abbot for an infringement of his rights concerning common of pasture at Uffculme. The King, however, intervened and issued an order proroguing 'until Friday the feast of St. Dennis (9 October) the taking of that Assize which they are proposing to take on Saturday next after scarce six days warning to the Abbot who is without Counsel, as that would tend to disherison of the Abbey, which is of the patronage of John, King of Castile and Duke of Lancastre'. The findings of the Court are unknown.

The middle of the 13th century was a time of some disorder when those who owned land of any size were claiming boundaries which did not exist or were not recognised by their neighbours. This appears to have been the situation between the Knights Hospitallers of the Order of St. John of Jerusalem and the Abbey. The Hospitallers, who had founded a religious house at Bodmescombe in A.D. 1160, were given two-and-a-half hides (about 300 acres) of land near their House at Bodmescombe on the north-west slopes of Sheldon Hill by Warin de Aula and Juliana his wife. Their land stretched along the wooded heights of Sheldon Hill and into Broadhembury. They were already established before the Abbey at Dunkeswell appeared in 1201 and both religious Houses had land adjoining each other but no clear boundaries. Disputes broke out and often developed into violent quarrels between the men of both Houses. These were settled by arbitration from time to time but finally a settlement was reached by Indentured agreement in the year 1253. On 29 September in that year the Prior and Brethren of St. John of Jerusalem agreed to

resign to the Abbey the Mill at Hembury and some other land including 80 acres of arable land at Ruffgreihay belonging to the Priory at Bodmescombe. The Abbey to pay the Prior £1.25p per annum and the Hospital resigned its claim to 35p rent from the Mill.

By another agreement not dated but probably near the same date the Prior of the Hospitallers agreed to

resign to the Abbey 3 ferlings (about 22 acres) of meadow at Catecombe and three parts of Cumbhangerwood (about 137 acres) consisting of moor and waste, once granted to the Hospitallers by Henry Fitzwilliam. The Abbey to pay an annual sum of 50p at Redscombe within the octave of Easter under a further penalty of £1. This agreement was made in the presence of the Abbot of Westminster and the Prior of Holy Trinity House, London.

The long-standing disputes between both Houses over the land boundaries was settled for the time being by the Abbey acquiring the land of the Hospitallers in return for annual payments. The Abbey gained about 250 acres of land and the Priory of the Hospitallers at Bodmescombe were reduced to a smaller acreage of land around their House at Bodmescombe. At this time the Priory of the Hospitallers was a small House containing only a handful of men, whose main purpose it was to train lads and pages for service overseas in the two Hospitals of the Order in Jerusalem, or for service in the military wing of the Order who were engaged in the Crusade against the Turks in the Holy Land. On the other hand the Cistercian Abbey at Dunkeswell had a vigorous community of some 70 or more lay and professed brethren eager to expand the agricultural activity of the Order. The Hospitallers had not the resources to bring much if any of the moor- and waste-land into cultivation whereas, the growing Cistercian Abbey was able to take this in its stride. The agreement seems a sensible arrangement because it gave the moor- and waste-land to the Cistercians who could bring it into cultivation, while the Hospitallers received an annual payment from the Abbey which continued for nearly 300 years to the dissolution in 1539.

Some 50 years or so later further disputes broke out between both Houses about the ownership and boundaries of land, when fights took place between the men of both Houses. The dispute this time was settled in a very different way. The Prior of the Hospitallers and the Abbot of Dunkeswell came to an agreement sometime between the years 1302 and 1327 in which it was admitted that the men of Dunkeswell were guilty of violence. The agreement stipulated that all the 'satellites' (men) of Dunkeswell Abbey who were present at the violence done to the men of the Priory were required on the 'sollum' day of the Feast of All Saints (1 November) to present themselves at the door of the House of the Hospitallers at Bodmescombe, stripped and barefoot, to be absolved, and that they should take corporate oath never henceforth to presume to sin against the brethren of the House of the Hospitallers. The Abbot of Dunkeswell was to satisfy R. and Walter, son of Alward de Heghes, men of the said Hospitallers, for injuries inflicted upon them, and acquit R. and Walter and their pledges before the Justice in Eyre (the Court) and save them indemnified in the King's Court because they were peaceful men. This dispute had probably been brought to a climax in the year 1327 when William de Quenton, the Vicar of Auliscombe (an impropriated Church of the Abbey) was found on the enclosed premises of the Prior of St. John's at Bodmescombe in an aggressive mood and armed (probably with a bow and arrows or a sword). William was summoned to appear at the King's Bench at Westminster charged with breaking into enclosed premises and being in possession of arms. Bishop Stapleton of Exeter was required to summon William to appear at the King's Court to answer the charge but the Bishop replied that he could not serve the writ as the Vicar was no longer under his jurisdiction. In other words, William had undoubtedly fled in the meantime and his whereabouts were unknown.

A final word about the Priory at Bodmescombe. Towards the end of the 14th century or early in the next, the Priory of the Hospitallers was absorbed into the Priory of Buckland, but the Chapel of the Priory was maintained at Bodmescombe into the 16th century. The land of the Hospitallers situated around the Priory was let out to farmers who in 1501 undertook to find a Chaplain for divine service at the Chapel and to provide him with a chamber, fuel and a stipend of 8 marks (£5.33p) a year with his food and raiment.

There was also disagreements over the right of common pasture on the Hill of Hembury and Hemburdowne situated north of the Abbey Grange there and the village of Broadhembury. Much of this land, if not all, had passed into the possession of the Abbey in the 13th. century and efforts were made to regularise its use as common pasture in the Manor. Robert de Somertone had land in the Manor and the Abbey by Indenture granted to Robert the right of common pasture there, and in return Robert by unsealed deed acknowledged that the Abbot had a right to build upon the Hill. Following is a copy of the unsealed deed:

15th July 1321: Whereas his very dear Lord the Abbot of the monastery of Dunkeswell and the Convent of the same place, by a certain writing indented, granted to Robert de Somertone common of pasture on Hemberdowne for all sorts of beasts at a fixed season; it shall be lawful for the Abbot and Convent, notwithstanding the common so granted, to build everywhere upon the said Hill whenever and how often soever they wish. Without disturbance of him or his men. (Hampshire R.O. Wriothesley Deed 48).

It is doubtful if Robert had the power to dispense the law in this way and the unsealed deed is probably an unofficial agreement between them that Robert would raise no objections if the Abbot built upon the common pasture on the Hill which in normal circumstances he was not entitled to do.

Did Roger de Somertone later join the Cistercian community at Dunkeswell Abbey? If he did he was soon in trouble, for seven years later, on 5 February 1328, the Bishop of Exeter excommunicated Brother Roger de Somertone, Monk of Dunkeswell, for failing to appear before him to answer some unspecified charges of crime or misdemeanour. The excommunication was lifted on 4 March but re-imposed for contempt on a day-to-day basis on 22 March. If Roger had joined the Cistercian community his land in Broadhembury would have passed into the possession of the Abbey. This is probably what happened, as a descendant of Robert de Somertone of the same name in 1470 claimed that dues payable to him by Abbey tenants at Puttingheys, Broadhembury were not being paid, and Abbot William agreed that he or his representative would in future attend the Manor Court at Broadhembury at Easter and Michaelmas each year and if the tenants failed to pay the dues and the Court decided they must be paid then, on every such occasion, the sum to be paid would be threepence ($1\frac{1}{4}$p) only for ever.

As time progressed much of the detailed work in the management of the Abbey Manors and estates was taken over by Bailiffs and Stewards – thus relieving the Abbot and his Chapter of much of the temporal burden they were carrying, and enabling them to expand the spiritual side of their lives – but the keeping of the King's Peace in most of the Manors belonging to the Abbey was a responsibility which could not so easily be disposed of.

The Abbot was the Keeper of the King's Peace and possessed the 'view of frankpledge' in the Manors of Lincumbe, Buckland Brewer, Hackpen, Dunkeswell and Broadhembury, and in each year an annual meeting of the Court Leat had to be held to which all villeins over the age of twelve were required to attend and register themselves. They were then constituted into groups of ten men, each group representing an area known as a 'tything'. The one in each tything who held the most land was appointed by the Court Leat as tythingman for the area and he was a kind of policeman who reported to the Manor Court regularly on the behaviour of the people in his 'tything'. In the case of violence every man in the group for that area was held responsible for apprehending the culprit and depositing him in the custody of the Court: if they failed to do so they were all liable to penalties. From the report of the tythingman the Manor Court meted out punishment for offences committed; for this purpose the Court erected stocks to secure offenders by the legs and pillories to secure them by the neck and wrists, and both were erected in public places so that the offenders could receive the abuse and derision of all who saw them. A more sinister instrument was the tumbrel – a tip-up cart – useful among other things for carrying convicted criminals to the gallows. The Abbots of Dunkeswell were responsible for some 300 years for keeping the King's Peace in the Manors where they had 'the view of frankpledge'.

The Manor Courts therefore over which the Abbot or his representative presided was an institution of major importance to all who lived within its jurisdiction. Attendance at its meetings was compulsory and, together with the Church, at which attendance was also compulsory, every aspect of life was ordered and controlled and obedience to its decrees enforced by fines and punishment. The only protection an individual had, if protection it can be called, was from custom as established by the long administration of affairs by

A 'hue and cry'

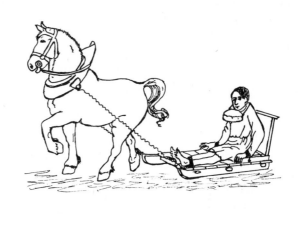

The baker taken to the pillory for selling short-weight loaves

the Manor Court. So long as the villein, bordar and cottar conformed to custom and observed their servile obligations they could not be dispossessed of the land they held, but they could be fined by the Court for such offences as cutting timber without permission, bad ploughing, failure to manure the land, growing the wrong crops, being late at Court, poaching and other misdemeanours.

The Manor Courts were served by paid servants of the Lord of the Manor, their number depending on the size of the Manor. If there was a bailiff of the Manor he was usually the Beadle of the Court responsible for summoning individuals to Court. He collected rents and Court fines and enforced servile duties on the Lord's desmesne which he also managed. A Hayward was usually appointed to supervise the pastures and the woodlands, the sowing of corn and the ploughing operations. Where a Reeve was appointed, he was a 'villein' nominated by the peasantry and usually appointed by the Lord and his job was to organise the duties of the villeins, bordars and cottars whom he could take to Court for avoiding service. He determined how the day's work should be carried out. For his services the Reeve received from the Lord certain privileges, including permission to graze his beasts upon the desmesne of the Lord and to receive a share of its crops. Very often the duties of all three were combined in one or two servants of the Lord depending upon the size of the Manor.

The 13th-century village was not a very desirable place in which to live, judged by our standards. The refinements of living were unknown and the dwellings mean and dirty. They were built with timber from the woods which provided a frame and the walls were of lathe plastered with clay kneaded with chopped straw. The floor was of bare earth over which a layer of straw or dried grass was strewn. From timbers in the ceiling a bacon rack was fixed from which hung pieces of cured bacon smoked from the timber fires burning on a clay hob. The smoke from the fire usually found its way out through a hole in the roof or the doorway. A ladder sometimes gave access to a sleeping-quarter overhead and beneath the thatched roof. Household refuse that could not be fed to the pig was thrown upon a heap outside the door where it stayed long enough to provide a festering source of infection. A hole in the ground with a pole across it or a seat placed over it with a roof of sorts to keep off the rain was the place where the family toilet was located.

This, then, is the picture of 13th-century life in the communities over which the Abbots of Dunkeswell presided.

CHAPTER FOUR

The Abbot's Powers. Fairs, Markets, Free warren

The Abbot's Powers. Fairs, Markets and Freewarren: The Seals of the Abbot and the Abbey. The King seizes two Manors. Subsidies to Pope and King. The Abbot's Treasurer. The system of Visitations. The Abbot's powers challenged – confirmed. Charter of Edward I – fairs, markets – free warren – their significance. Medieval society.

IN THE early years the management and financing of the Conventual activity was done by the professed brethren over whom the Abbot presided at their daily Chapter meeting. As time went on, however, the Chapter became quite unequal to the task with the result that many, if not most, Houses got themselves into a mess and became heavily in debt. They were often taken advantage of by outsiders who had business connections with the Convent and when matters became hopeless the Patron, King or Bishop intervened. Sometimes the Chapter itself rose to the occasion but where the responsibility for the chaos lay with an incompetent Abbot it was almost impossible to bring about a change because of the reverence bestowed upon his person by the community. The corporate authority of the community was represented by the Abbot who possessed a Seal with which he could do away with the Abbey land and property by using it upon documents without the knowledge and consent of the Chapter. When debts and other liabilities piled up there was no other way of paying them except to sell the land. So widespread did this practice become that Edward I, just before his death in 1306–7, instituted the Statute of Carlisle which very effectively brought to an end the power of the Abbots in the use of their Seals. The Statute declared that every Religious House should have a Common Seal to be kept in the custody of the Prior and four of the most worthy and discreet men of the House. The Seal was to be placed in safe keeping under the private Seal of the Abbot. This meant that the Abbot could not use his own Seal upon legal documents and that the Common Seal could only be used with the consent of at least five other members of the community. The King directed that the Statute must be read openly and recited twice a year in full Chapter of the House under the pains and penalties in the Statute for failure to do this.

Impression of the seal of John, Abbot of St Mary's
Abbey, Dunkeswell, some time between 1235–49
(original size, 1 × 1⅝ in.)

The only known Seal of an Abbot of Dunkeswell is that from an impression attached to a Charter and now in the Public Record Office in London under reference DL/25/214. Its survival is due to the fact that it was preserved in the early records of the Duchy of Lancaster whose Dukes were the Patron of the Abbey. It was used sometime between the years 1235–49 by Abbot John to seal the Charter he gave to Sir Payn de Chaureys indemnifying him from any liability to pay the Feudal dues to the King on the land of the Manor of Lincumbe. This Manor was given to the Abbey by the founder, Lord William Brewer, shortly before he died in 1226 and the Charter stated that the gift was free of all feudal dues and exactions, which meant that the donor and not the Abbey would pay the dues to the King. The same condition applied to Buckland Brewer inherited by the Abbey from William Brewer, the son of the founder who died in 1233. However, the donor's successors had not paid the dues to the King, who seized both Manors pending consideration of the matter by the King's Bench. On 3 November 1235 the Abbot was summoned to appear in London to explain why he had not paid the feudal dues. As the loss of revenue of both Manors was a serious matter for the Abbey the Abbot journeyed to Winchester where the King was staying for Xmas, and on Boxing Day, 26 December 1235, he secured an audience with the King and asked that

Fragment of the seal impression of Dunkeswell Abbey as used on the instrument of surrender to Henry VIII on 14 February 1539 (actual size). The official description of the seal is, 'Painted red oval, the Virgin standing in carved and canopied niche between two smaller canopied niches, each containing a saint, full length. In the interior hand a book and in the exterior hand a pastoral staff. In base under a round-headed arch the Abbot, with pastoral staff, between two shields of arms: left – wanting; right – two bands wavy' (the latter was the arms of the founder)

one third of a carucate (40 acres) of land with appurtenances in each of the Manors of Lincumbe and Buckland Brewer be released to him on bail pending a settlement. The King's Bench decided that the Abbot must pay the feudal dues on both Manors and the successors of William Brewer and his son indemnified of any such liability.

The revenues of the Abbey were not audited in the earlier period and gifts of land and property were often for specific purposes rather than for the general purposes of the House as a whole. These gifts were handed over to which ever Obedientary it was in charge of that kind of activity and the revenue became his to do with practically as he pleased, and the Abbot had little control over it. The Abbot, however, was responsible for the general expenses of his House including the payment of taxes both secular and ecclesiastical. There was no general form of taxation levied by the Crown at this time and when the King needed money for a particular purpose he devised a special levy upon a special group or body of individuals and none knew upon whom the blow would fall next. The records of Newenham Abbey tell us that in 1276 Edward I decided to levy the Cistercian Houses the sum of £1,000 to maintain his expedition against Llewellyn, the Prince of Wales, whose defeat the following year brought an end to the independence of Wales. The sum levied upon Dunkeswell Abbey was £14.67p. For those times this sum was a substantial amount to demand. Another sample of the demands made by the King from time to time was that in June 1332, when he asked for a subsidy in aid of the expenses incurred for the marriage of his sister Eleanor to Reginald, the Count of Guelders, and he sent John de Bruxton to Dunkeswell Abbey to collect it. Successive Kings seemed to have regarded the Abbeys as an almost limitless source of revenue as tax after tax was levied to meet all kinds of royal purposes, from wars to dowers for the King's female relatives in marriage.

The Pope, too, from time to time levied taxes and loans upon the Religious Houses and sometimes accompanied them with threats of ex-communication. In 1240 the Papal Legate Otho summoned the heads of Religious Houses to London and demanded from them large sums to help finance the Pope's war against the Emperor Frederick, but this was refused him. Later that year and before Otho returned to Rome he called the Religious Houses to another meeting and, assisted by the King, persuaded the monastic Heads to find the money asked for and all agreed except the Cistercians, who refused to pay. In 1254 the Pope gave the King a tenth of the income of all ecclesiastical property and in the following year his Legate Rustard arrived, summoned the Heads of Religious Houses to London and demanded so large a sum of money from them that it would have ruined them to have paid it. The Heads refused to find the money. The King and the Legate were very angry and they sought other means the following year to raise money by making individual demands upon selected monasteries. It was said the collusion of the King and the Pope to extract money from the Religious Houses was like the wolf and the shepherd together harassing the fold, each trying all he knew how to take as much money from them as they could. To add to the problem, the ever open door of hospitality, abused as it was, became a very heavy drain upon the revenues of the Abbey.

It is no wonder that many monastic Houses were in financial difficulties as it would have taxed the ingenuity of the most competent Abbot to have kept his House on an even financial keel in the midst of all those pressures to undermine it. The financial transactions involved in the running of the Abbey estates, in financing its services together with the demands for money by the Pope and King needed some degree of accurate accountancy and supervision. But there was none at this time apart from the attention a harassed Abbot could give. To help him, Abbot William brought in a layman as his 'Treasurer', but he in turn found it almost impossible to consolidate the income and expenditure of the House as a whole. The independence of the Obedientaries could not be overcome and the treasurers found they could not achieve what was expected of them. Abbot William in 1326 had difficulty in obtaining from his Treasurer William Vyncent a statement of accounts and took him to Court to exact a statement from him. He, poor fellow, sent a mesage to Court to say that he was hoping to be able to do this after some delay.

The Cistercian Houses were exempted from visitation by the Bishop because it was thought the Cistercian system of visitation was sufficient. That system provided for a three-yearly visitation of each House in England by a representative of the General Chapter of the Mother Abbey at Citeaux, and an annual visitation to the daughter House by the founding Mother House – which in the case of Dunkeswell was the Abbey of Forde. Between them they had absolute power to correct abuses, make changes in administration and even to depose Obedientaries and the Abbot himself for incompetence. This system of dual supervision proved quite inadequate as time passed, visitations became less frequent and the scope for abuse widened. There is no evidence that Dunkeswell was ever a disorderly House although at times it must have reflected to some extent the state of society outside the precincts. The management and administration of the affairs of the Abbey in the later period was much improved by the employment of Stewards and Bailiffs to manage the estates and an Auditor to take care of its financial activity.

When Edward I ascended the throne in 1272 he found the revenues of the Crown, during the reign of his father Henry III, had considerably diminished through tenants-in-chief alienating their land without the King's license, by witholding from the Crown under various pretexts its just rights and by the usurpation of the right of holding Court and other legal processes. Numerous sanctions and oppressions of the people had been committed in the reign of Henry III by the nobility and gentry claiming the rights of free chase, free warren and fishery, demanding unreasonable tolls at fairs and markets and by Sheriffs, Escheators and other officers and ministers under the colour of law. There was a complete breakdown of administration and the new King set about the restoration of law and order, first by appointing Special Commissioners to enquire into these matters and to report back to him. Juries were empanelled in the Hundreds and the towns to collect evidence upon oath of occupation of any office, franchise or liberty, as well as oppressions and illegal exactions; and upon the information so gathered the King's Justices in Eyre went on circuit throughout the country and issued writs summoning persons to appear before them to show by what authority their rights and claims were supported. The Abbot of Dunkeswell was served with such a writ in 1281 and he had to appear before the Justices to prove his right to exercise the powers of 'frankpledge' – that is, the right of the Abbots of Dunkeswell through their Manorial Courts to supervise the behaviour of local people and other ancient rights of ownership in the Manors of Hembury (Broadhembury) Hackpen (Uffculme), Buckland Brewer, Lincumbe and Dunkeswell, as well as the right to set up gallows there and to levy fines on the making of bread and ale; and to explain similar claims in the Manor of Coleton (Collaton Raleigh). The Justices had before them the reports of the Juries set up by the Hundred Courts which covered the Manors concerned. The Hundred Court of Hayridge reported that they had appointed twelve Jurors to enquire into the rights of the Abbot's of Dunkeswell in Hembury. They stated upon oath that the Abbots held the Manor of Hembury in free and perpetual gift from William Brewer and that the same Abbots possessed the gallows and the assize of corn, bread and beer belonging to the Manor from ancient times and from the confirmation of John and the present King's father Henry.

There were similar reports from the other Hundred Courts.

The Abbot appeared however before Salamon de Ross and his fellow Justices in Eyre at Exeter on the Octave of St. Martyn (18 November) 1281 to prove his entitlement to the rights claimed. The record of the event is as follows:

The Abbot came. As to the gallows, he said he had rights (*infangenthef* and *utfangenethef* — Saxon terms for the judging of robbers taken within their liberties with stolen goods) in Coleton and Hembury dated from the Charter granted by King John, the present King's forebear. As for the view of frankpledge which he claimed, the Abbot declared that the same King had granted him and his men, by the aforesaid Charter exemption from all secular taxes and aids in the Shire and Hundreds. He added by the same warrant he claimed the right of 'frank pledge' for observing the King's Peace and that his men were not compelled to answer for their actions to any other men . . . (Placita Quo Warranto Rot. 39d. Edw. I.)

The King's representative, William de Gyselham, thought this was an unreasonable claim and judgement upon it was deferred.

It was not until the year 1285 that the King allowed the Abbot's claim but not until he explained why he did not allow the men of his tything at Coleton (Collaton Raleigh) to attend the Hundred Court of the King at Buddelegh. The Abbot replied that the King's grandfather King John, and the King's father King Henry, had granted the Abbey a Charter decreeing that the Abbot should possess his men and servants, land, tenements and whatever other tenements he should acquire in the future in perpetual freedom and safe and immune from all secular service of Shire and Hundred. The King postponed the matter *sine die* and the Abbot therefore continued to exercise his rights and powers.

Five years later the King granted the Abbey a Charter of some significance. It was dated 4 August 1290 and reads:

Grant to the Abbot and Convent of Donekwell of two weekly markets on Wednesday, one at the Manor of Boclande Bruer and the other at Brodehembury, Co. Devon and of two yearly fairs at the same Manors on the Vigil, Feast and the morrow of the Assumption of St. Mary (14th, 15th and 16th of August), grant also of free warren in all their desmesne lands in the Manors of Boclande Bruer, Brodehembiri, Sobbecombe, Wringeston, Hakpenne, Uggaton, Hawkerlond, Dodeton (Collaton Raleigh), Buwewode, Bolham, Auliscombe, Wulferchurche, Burehays, Bywode, Scilden (Sheldon), Steyntwode and Ullecombe (Lincumbe) Co., Devon.

This grant was undoubtedly purchased by the Abbey from the King. There were not many monasteries that had grants of markets and fairs. They brought substantial advantages to the Abbey as also did the granting of 'free warren' in the desmesne lands. Having regard to their importance in the lives of the people upon the Abbey estates it is necessary to consider what these powers involved.

The grant of 'free warren' meant, in a legal sense, that in all the land of the Abbey except land let to free tenants, the Abbot had the exclusive right to the wild animals, birds and fish on that land or in any pond or river, and no other person was entitled to take or hunt them, except in the case of deer which were 'beasts of the forest' and not 'beasts of the warren' like foxes, hares, rabbits, and which, with pheasants, pigeons, doves and a host of other animals and birds were then plentiful. As there were in most cases no boundaries or clearly defined limits of a warren, which was an open area in or bordering upon a large area of open waste, it was difficult to enforce the law and so the villagers found ways and means on occasion to take some wild animals, birds and fish, but if they were caught doing so they were taken before the Manor or Hundred Court and fined. Sometimes the Lord of the Manor would permit a certain amount of hunting for wild animals, birds and fish on payment of a sum of money for the right to do so in a specified area only. Pigeons and doves were often domesticated by the Lord as an important supply of food for his household and for this purpose pigeon-lofts and dovecotes were erected and from these each morning there issued forth sometimes hundreds of birds which promptly descended upon the cultivated corn-lands of the peasants and devoured the ripening corn. The peasant had no redress against the Lord who was fattening the birds for his table at the expense of the peasants. Likewise the rabbit was permitted to devour the peasants' crops. The only way the peasant could retaliate was to set down snares and traps of various kinds to reduce the number of the predators and, incidentally, provide himself with a tasty though unlawful meal. If the offender was caught he was liable to be heavily fined. Although the Abbots as Lords of the Manors sought always to retain their rights, it is doubtful if they were as rapacious in their attitude to their peasantry as were their lay counterparts. The Abbots were always generous to those who served the Abbey and there is little doubt that they had an understanding with their peasantry about 'free warren' which was unlikely to apply to outsiders.

The grant of weekly markets on Wednesdays and an annual fair in August at Buckland Brewer and Broadhembury indicates an important development in the activities of the Abbey in those areas. The growth of population there was breaking out of the isolation and the self-sufficiency of the village and stretching out its hands for contact and exchange with other communities. Agricultural production had increased substantially and there was now a measure of surplus over and above that required by the village, and so a market would provide an outlet for its disposal as well as the purchasing power for acquiring other useful and necessary things. The weekly markets were sited at cross-roads which were convenient for a number of manorial settlements

and here were brought cattle, sheep and other animals and farm products surplus to requirements, and which were bought by buyers engaged in supplying
the growing towns with food supplies. Some craftsmen brought articles of
clothing and household utensils which found ready buyers among the rural
communities. The markets were organised by the Cellarer of the Abbey with
the aid of the local steward or bailiff, and tolls were levied upon those who
made use of the markets to dispose of their stock and products. The Abbey,
however, was the principal beneficiary of the market as this provided a ready
outlet for the sale of livestock and farm products from the Abbey Manors.

The Fairs, however, were rather different events held annually and sited outside the townships of Buckland Brewer and Broadhembury, it being borne in
mind that the 'township' in those days was little more than a large village,
growing nevertheless. The Fairs were also organised by the Cellarer of the
Abbey together with the local officials of the Abbey Manors and payments
were made by those who required a booth, stall, tent, pitch or otherwise displayed wares for sale. The tolls were known as lastage, payage, frontage and
stallage and were levied upon the total taken from sales. A wide variety of
people came to the fair from miles around and included noble and serf, church-
man and soldier, merchant, trader, peasant, monk and craftsman. The goods
and articles offered were a wide variety such as linen, cloth, leather, grain, furs,
skins, kitchen and household vessels, iron and brass articles, tar in barrels for
the treatment of foot-rot and skin disease in sheep, oil wax, salt and pepper,
salt-fish and herrings for salting down for winter eating. Normally these things
could not be obtained locally except at Fairs, and so the Cellarers of Religious
Houses and Lords of the Manor and others found this a source of supply of
necessities which they could not supply themselves but which could be bought
at the Fair and stored until required. The Fairs were also attended by
Apothecaries who usually did a roaring trade selling remedies and potions for
all the ills that the body of man and animals are subject to. The pedlars and
chapmen displayed their wares and men dealing in hides and skins, and iron
(usually sold in 4 lb. bars — $1\frac{3}{4}$kg) were in attendance. Merchants also came from
other parts seeking orders for supplies, and as time went on foreign imports
found their way on to the stalls and foreign merchants came to buy mostly
wool for export. In addition, of course, there was the fun of the fair in games,
plays, sideshows, music by minstrels, displays by gymnasts and others, so that
a good time was had by all on August 14th, 15th and 16th each year at
Buckland Brewer and Broadhembury — two centres which covered a wide area
of manorial settlements.

Having regard to the large number of people who gathered at the fairs and
markets and the growing volume of trading which took place there the Abbot,
through his appropriate Manor Court, established a system of weights and

measures to be observed by all who took part. There were at times arguments between the rustic wayfarer and the seller as to price but, like the oriental market of today, there was no hurry to conclude a bargain. If disagreement about price led to blows, as it sometimes did, there was at hand the Abbot's Judges who not only arbitrated on the price to be paid but saw to it that the prices fixed by the Manor Court for bread, corn and ale were observed. The 'Judges' also kept the peace and brought any offenders before the Manorial

A fourteenth-century fair

Court if they were minor cases, or the Hundred Court if they were serious ones; but there were times when the large concourse of people was used as a cover for conspiratorial activity against the Church and State. The Abbot, endowed with the power of keeping the King's Peace, was responsible for law and order.

The attitude of the Cistercians towards markets and fairs was laid down by the General Chapter at Citeaux, who thought it inconsistent with their spiritual ideals of renunciation of the secular world that they should take part in them, but the Abbots, as Lords of Manors, had a public duty which they could not ignore. Besides, the active role they played in agriculture propelled them inevitably towards a system of marketing their agricultural products that was

Juggler

Selling hawks

irresistible. However, an elaborate code of behaviour was laid down for those who had to take part in markets and fairs. They were not to trade in any sense except to sell only the Abbey produce and this was to be carried out honestly and fairly. No more than two monks or conversi were to be sent from the Abbey to a market or fair and they were not to remain there longer than three or four days. They were required to carry or purchase their own sustenance and were forbidden to seek this for themselves or their horses from any other Religious House. If their food was purchased, they must not buy fish or delicacies and only well-watered wine. Trading was strictly forbidden unless it was connected with Abbey requirements and then they were warned against concealing defects in what they offered for sale and buying goods at a low price to sell at a higher price and raising the price if payment was deferred: usury must be avoided at all costs. The Abbey could send two professed or conversi Monks to markets and fairs other than their own and one of the two was usually the Cellarer who, with his horse and cart, relied more and more upon the

A minstrel troupe

markets and fairs to dispose of the surplus and buy in the necessities which in turn maintained the momentum of the life of the community. At this time the markets and fairs were of limited and local importance but they grew with time into very active and important elements in the agricultural economy, and with the corresponding growth of a money economy the brave attempts of the General Chapter at Citeaux to preserve the purity of Cistercian doctrine slowly subsided before the rising tide of commercial activity.

CHAPTER FIVE

Life in the Abbey

THE ABBOT was the head of the Monastery, absolute ruler and father of the community, and was treated with great reverence. He could appoint or depose any officer under him except the Prior – for whose dismissal he had to secure the consent of the convent. In the early period he and the Prior slept in the dortor and ate in the frater with the brethren, but later they had separate accommodation which enhanced the dignity of their offices. The Abbot had a 'lodging' where he ate, slept and kept some retainers. He was very fully occupied with the affairs of the Abbey and the State, and he became a great landowner and the equal of nobility, and upon his frequent travels whether near or far he was accompanied by a retinue which often included a nobleman's son sent to him for education. A despotic Abbot could override any rules and frustrate the efforts of his subordinates to maintain efficiency and economy in the running of the Abbey, with the result that the state of the Abbey often reflected the competence or otherwise of the Abbot.

Only the head of the Cistercian Order at Citeaux or the Pope had the power to depose an Abbot, though the Bishop could ex-communicate him for disorderly conduct. The Abbot, being a feudal grandee, could use the courts to fight for what he considered his rights. There were others, however, who welcomed the opportunity of being relieved from what they considered too great a burden.

Normally the Abbacy became vacant by death, by transfer of the Abbot to another House or by abdication. Before a new Abbot could be appointed a licence had to be obtained from the founder or the patron who had legal custody of temporal affairs during the vacancy. The licence having been obtained the election was then supervised by the Abbot of Forde – the Mother Abbey of Dunkeswell. The first step in the election process was taken by the acting head of the community, usually the Prior or a senior brother, who summoned the brethren to an assembly to fix a day for electing a new Abbot. A candidate for the office was expected to be well educated and have capacity for management in his subordinate offices before election. He should possess skill in managing his House and its estates and hold his own in defending the rights and privileges of the Abbey in the Courts against attempts made to filch away those rights and prerogatives. When the day for the election had been fixed notices were sent out to all concerned, including the Apostolic notary whose job it was to take note of all that happened that day. On the day appointed for the election the brethren were summoned to Church by the tolling of the great bell for the Mass *de Spirita Sancto* at the end of which, in procession, they went to the Chapter House. Here a short instruction about procedure was given by a senior member of the community and the names of the brethren who had the right to vote were called over by the presiding member. Then they chanted a hymn *Veni Creator Spiritas*, after which the presiding member in the name of God, charged that anyone excommunicated, suspended or interdicted and any others not entitled to vote by law and custom to be present, must depart forthwith so that the community may, in perfect freedom, proceed to the election. The founder or the patron's license was then read out and the constitution governing the election read. There were three possible ways of election. First, by vote of all those present and entitled to vote; any not present to sign a statement on oath saying why they were absent and appointing a proxy for them. Secondly, by the Chapter delegating to a small number of members the power to make an election. Thirdly, by divine inspiration – that is by all unanimously and spontaneously acclaiming a certain person.

When the election was over *Te Deum* was sung and the new Abbot was carried or conducted to the steps of the High Altar in the Lady Chapel from where the choice of the Chapter was proclaimed. The new Abbot was formally requested to give his consent to acceptance of the office, and the whole proceedings of the election was written up in a report by the Apostolic notary for submission to the founder or patron and to the Bishop of Exeter for approval and confirmation – only a formality if the election had been properly conducted. The new Abbot had then to proceed to the Bishop of Exeter to obtain confirmation and blessing, as this could not be done in the Abbey Church. It could, however, take place wherever the Bishop happened to be at the time. For instance, Abbot John was blessed at Yarcombe Parish Church on 17 October 1311 by the Bishop of Exeter. The procedure was that the Abbot took an oath of obedience to the Bishop, which he then signed and this was placed upon the Altar when the Abbot received the Bishop's blessing. The Diocesan authorities then levied a charge upon the Abbey for the confirmation and benediction, the Vicar General's confirmation and for ecclesiastical registration, which totalled £31.97p.

The next step was the Abbot's induction into office and a day was appointed for this. On that day at the tolling of the bell the Abbot walked barefoot to the Church door and after a suitable pause was received by the community, who conducted him to the High Altar where he lay prostrate on the ground while *Te Deum* was chanted. At the conclusion he was conducted to his seat and the proceedings of his election and confirmation were read out. The brethren then, one by one, knelt before their new Abbot and received from him the kiss of peace. The Abbot was regarded as the father and the representative of Christ in their midst and henceforth all were to stand and bow to him as he passed by. In the Refectory and Chapter House none was to sit until the Abbot was seated.

The type of ship that took the abbots of Dunkeswell from Dover to Calais to attend the General Chapter at Citeaux

In the cloister, unless invited by the Abbot to do so, no one must sit next to him and if the Abbot was speaking no one must break into his talk with remarks of their own. Familiarity with the Abbot was to be avoided at all costs as one would wish to avoid familiarity with the Almighty himself. The Abbot took the leading part in all Church services if he was present and in his absence the Prior took his place. He read the gospel at Matins, gave the blessing, offered the Holy Sacrifice of the Mass at the Great Altar and presided at Chapter meetings.

The Abbots of Dunkeswell were very busy men who carried a heavy load, especially in early times when the Abbey was under construction and the Manors needed close attention. In addition much time was spent in travelling to Citeaux to attend the annual General Chapter of the Order; to London to attend the Convocation of the Clergy; to Exeter for Diocesan business. The visits to Citeaux were always undertaken under the protection of the King and typical of many entries in the Patent Rolls is the following: '1st July 1285: Protection, with clause volumus, until All Saints (1st November) for the Abbot of Donekeswell going beyond the seas'. '20th July 1302: Simple protection until Easter for the Abbot of Donkyswylle, going beyond the seas'.

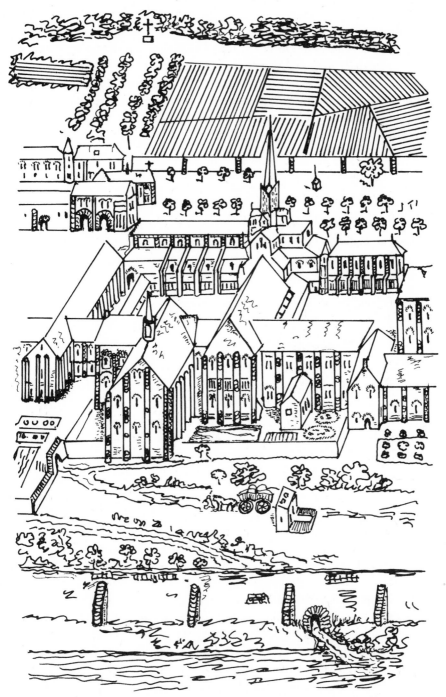

The Abbey of Citeaux (from an old engraving)

These journeys to Citeaux were annual events in the early period but were taken less frequently as time went on. The Abbot went accompanied by a retinue on horseback to Dover to await a suitable wind, tide and boat to take them across to Calais and thence they proceeded on horseback to Citeaux in central France. The Abbot was accustomed to take money and gifts to the Mother Abbey from her grand-daughter Abbey at Dunkeswell, but at a later date the King took action to prevent the passing of money and gifts in this way. On 9 February 1302 he made this order:

An Order of the King prohibiting the Abbot of Dunkewelle (and other Cistercian Abbots) from sending out of the realm any money by gift or exchange, loan or otherwise. It had come to the King's notice that the Abbot of Citeaux had sent proctors to the Abbot of Rievaulx to exact a quantity of money for the use of the Abbot of Citeaux. (Close Rolls Bk. 13. p 576).

In 1308 it appears that the Abbot of Dunkewelle and some other Cistercian Abbots attended the General Chapter at Citeaux without the King's permission and on their return they were arrested by the Constable of Dover and detained pending the King's direction. This he indicated as follows:

4 October 1308: An order to Robert de Kendale, Constable of Dover and Warden of the Cinque Ports ordering him to release the Abbot of Dunkeswelle (and others of the Cistercian Order) whom he had arrested because they passed the sea without the King's license to attend the General Chapter at Citeaux. (Close Rolls Bk. 15. p 19)

From now on Cistercian Abbots could not travel to their Mother Abbey in the free way that they did by purchasing the King's protection. Now they had to purchase a licence which imposed restrictions and prohibited the taking of money and gifts. Without the licence they could not visit Citeaux so they had to bow to the restrictions. But the visits continued as the following entry in the Close Rolls show:

24 July 1334: To the Keeper of the Port of Dover, Order to permit the Abbot of Dunkewelle of the Cistercian Order, who is about to set out by the King's license to his Chapter General at Citeaux, to cross from that port to those parts with £10 for his expenses and those of his household. (Close Rolls Bk. 20. p 326)

The link between the Abbey and Citeaux gradually weakened over the years until finally it was broken by Henry VIII. As the clouds gathered overhead and destruction threatened, the Cistercian Abbots appealed to their Mother House at Citeaux to send to them a visitor. Citeaux sent them a monk who arrived in London in 1531 but the King refused to allow him to visit the Cistercian Abbeys although he had a perfect juridical right to do so. The King alleged 'that no one had a right to interfere in the affairs of his Kingdom, saying that he was at once King, Emperor and Pope in his dominions'.

The Abbot regularly attended the Convocation of the Clergy usually held annually but often irregularly at St. Paul's in London.

The Bishop of Exeter nominated those who were to attend from his Diocese and this always included the Abbots of Dunkeswell. The Convocations usually lasted for three weeks and sometimes longer. It was the Convocation which decided how much ecclesiastical benefices would pay in tax to the King. This usually took the form of a tax of one tenth upon the value or income of land and property and the Abbots of Dunkeswell, by direction of the Bishop, took their turn in collecting this tax from the ecclesiastical benefices in Devon and paying it into the King's Exchequer through the Sheriff of the County.

The Abbot had a town-house in Exeter situated in St. Paul's Parish and here he took up residence on occasions when he had business with the diocesan authorities. The Abbot also had a house and garden of some size in Honiton which he undoubtedly used in the administration of the substantial estates belonging to the Abbey in the nearby parishes of Giddesham, Buckerell and Auliscombe. These estates adjoined the boundaries and most probably were part of the township of Honiton on the south and the west parts of the present town.

The Abbots never left the Abbey without being accompanied by a retinue of servants and, depending upon the occasion, one or more Knights whose duty it was to protect the Abbot and care for his personal needs. Travelling was by horseback. Periodically it was the Abbot's duty to visit his Manors including those at Lincumbe, Buckland Brewer and Collaton Abbot where he undoubtedly stayed overnight. The medieval Abbots therefore were on the move for much of the year but when they were not they were busily engaged in consultations with their Obedientaries about the organisation of Abbey affairs. Few of them escaped financial worries arising from their own incompetence, or the incompetence of their Obedientaries; from bad harvests, floods, civil disturbances and excessive taxation by Rome and the King. Living on credit and borrowed money was an accepted way of life in the Middle Ages and the piling up of debts was a legitimate way of overcoming losses. Now and then a strong Abbot would come to the top, clear the debts and restore financial solvency, but his successors were always liable to take the easy road to insolvency again.

The Prior was acting Head of the Abbey when the Abbot was absent. He was appointed by the Abbot but he could not be dismissed without the consent of the community. The Prior was therefore second in authority to the Abbot and had special duties allocated to him which were established by rule and custom. He had the responsibility for maintaining internal discipline and for the spiritual life of the House. The rule says the Prior must be 'remarkable for his holiness', overflowing in charity and abundant sympathy and act in a way as the mother of the community as the Abbot was the father and the brethren his sons. He must be loved and not feared and regarded as an angel of peace. He must root out evil tendencies and be unwearied in his labours, tender to those in trouble and set himself an example to the brethren. He was to chastise the rebellious, encourage the timid, sustain the weak and be long suffering himself and a physician of the soul. He should also have the patience of Job and the devotion of David. These were all formidable qualities to expect in one man and it is doubtful if ever one was found to possess them all, but the Prior was universally honoured. When he came to Chapter and Collation all stood until he had taken his seat.

The Cellarer was the most important of all the Obedientaries and was appointed by the Abbot who could also displace him. In practice, however, the Abbot and the Cellarer frequently acted together on their own responsibility in deciding matters of great importance. The Cellarer's establishment was situated conveniently opposite the Gatehouse to receive supplies entering the precincts and he did the buying and selling of land and property and supervised the leases granted by the Abbot. The Granges, manors, farms and other property were in his change as also were the Abbey mills, malthouses, brewhouses and transport. He directed the labour of the conversi and engaged, dismissed and punished any servants. The provision of food, drink, fuel and the granaries were in his charge. His ability determined the prosperity and smooth running of the corporate affairs of the Abbey. He was often away at the Granges, manors, markets and fairs procuring supplies for the Abbey and selling live-stock, surplus grain and other crops. There was considerable temptation to become a man of the world rather than a cloistered Monk. Men of ability for discharging an office of this kind were far from plentiful and the allocation of these duties to a brother esteemed for his devout piety often brought debt and confusion in its train. The Cellarers usually had an assistant who, the Rule said, must be obliging, cheerful, moderate in his manners and courteous to strangers and capable of bearing hard words from others and to hand out a gentle and soft reply. He shared responsibility with the Kitchener to see that meals were properly prepared and promptly served. In providing bread for the convent he must see that it was not dirty, broken or burnt; beer must not be supplied unless it was more than four days old. The gardener of the Abbey was under his charge and this person was responsible for seeing that the House was regularly supplied with fruit, vegetables and herbs from the garden. A full range of herbs were to be made available to the Infirmary where their healing properties were in regular demand. In later years the appointment of Stewards and Bailiffs relieved the Cellarer of much of his responsibility for the Manors and Granges.

The Almoner too was an Obedientary appointed by the Abbot who could also dismiss him. He had charge of the charitable activity of the Abbey and his Almonry was situated at or near the Gatehouse where poor guests were lodged and poor people came daily for the distribution of food which was regularly made by the monks. Here too was the place where boys were taught and maintained by the Abbey. The Almoner was expected to possess certain characteristics which were laid down. He must be a God-fearing man, kind and compassionate and discreet in the distribution of largesse to pilgrims, palmers, chaplains, beggars and lepers. He was required to pay frequent visits to decrepit old men, the lame and the blind who were bedridden and to suitably relieve them. Any woman present at this time had to leave before the Almoner could enter the room. He was not to attend upon sick women but one of his servants must take what was necessary to them. The Almoner must endure with calmness any loud-voiced pleadings of destitute people, and in no case must he strike or injure them but he should answer them with moderation and patience. At the feet-washing ceremony on Thursdays in the cloister alley the Almoner had the duty of finding the poor men whose feet were to be washed by the Monks and he had to arrange to collect from the frater daily the left-over

The daily distribution of food to the old and the sick

food from meals there for feeding to the poor lodged in the Almonry, and to collect discarded clothing for distribution to them. He must also prevent intruders from entering the cloister and keep it clean and tidy as well as the quarters of the sick, the floors of which were to be strewn with fresh hay or straw.

The Chamberlain, appointed and dismissed by the Abbot, had little contact with lay folk outside the Abbey. His duties were internal and domestic. He had charge of the dortors or sleeping-places of the conversi and the professed and his duties were meticulously laid down. He was to provide straw mattresses once a year on which occasions the dortors were to be thoroughly cleaned up. In the cloister he had to provide warm water for shaving, soap for washing and baths for the brethren usually three or four times a year. Around the tubs in which the bath-water was placed he must scatter sweet hay for the brethren to stand upon. For the feet-washing ceremony on Saturday evenings the Chamberlain had to provide hot water and a good fire in the common room for this occasion when the cooks washed the feet of the brethren. This must not be confused with the washing of poor men's feet on Thurdays by the Abbot, and the poor children's feet by the monks, in separate locations in the cloister alleys and at the end of which the poor men and children were given food and money. The Chamberlain also had to arrange for the shaving of heads every two or three weeks in the cloister by a barber surgeon who was probably a monk. On these occasions the brethren formed themselves into two rows facing each other in seniority order. The senior heads were shaved first 'when the razors are sharp and towels dry' and by the time the juniors and novices were reached the water was cold and the towels wet. The Chamberlain provided the clothing for the brethren and from the conversi came the tailors who made up the cloth and did the repairs to the garments of the community. The Chamberlain travelled by horse-and-cart to neighbouring markets and fairs to buy cloth, leather and other materials required and these he brought back to the House to be made up by the conversi tailors, shoemakers and seamsters. He also bought lambskins and catskins which were cured and used to line winter garments worn by the brethren at night in Church offices. Other purchases included towels, sheets, soap etc., and from the conversi came the launderers who washed the linen, surplices, rochets, sheets, shirts, drawers and anything else usually once a fortnight in summer and once in three weeks in winter.

The Sacrist and the Precentor were Obedientaries whose duties were almost wholly connected with the Church. The Sacrist was responsible for the Church, its contents and its treasure, while the Precentor was in charge of arrangements for and the management of the services in Church as well as the Processionals which were an important part of monastic life. While the Sacrist maintained the cleanliness and repair of the Church and its altars and shrines

Dunkeswell Abbey: reconstructed from a sketch made by the Rev. John Swete in 1794. The building – probably a guest house or accommodation for lay persons serving the abbey – was north-west of the Conventual Church; the stream flows north-east. Below, a guest and a pilgrim.

the Precentor saw that all those taking part in the services understood them and properly performed them, himself being the chief singer and leader. He was, too, the Librarian and had charge of the books including those in use in the Church. He held one of the keys of the Abbey Chest containing the records of the Abbey and he was one of the five who held a key giving access to the Abbey Seal.

The Guest House played an important part in the life of the Abbey at a time when there were no inns or hotels. This was a period when long pilgrimages were made to sacred shrines and holy places and the pilgrim could always rely upon free hospitality in a monastic Guest House. If Guests were in residence at the time of special religious services on a Saint's Feast Day they were invited to attend the services. They could also attend Matins if they wished, when the Hosteller with his lantern took them to the Church, found them a place and a book and a light to read by. After Matins the Hosteller brought them back to the Guest House and to their beds to resume their broken sleep. Poor guests however were lodged in the Almonry.

It was the custom of the feudal nobility, when it suited them, to descend upon a monastery with a retinue and park themselves down as guests until it pleased them to move on. The principal guests were entertained by the Abbot in a special suite and their retainers were accommodated in the Guest House. Provision also had to be made for the stabling and feeding of the horses of the guests. This became a very heavy burden which brought some monasteries near to bankruptcy. Payment for the hospitality could not be demanded and although some made a contribution towards the burden others did not. The King for instance pensioned off his servants by billeting them upon the monasteries who received no payment towards the cost.

The school for boys held a place of some importance in the activities of the community. The boys came from some families to whom the Abbey had granted carrodies for gifts of land, some from poor families living upon nearby Abbey manors, while others were the sons of freemen and the gentry. There was no class distinction in the school and each boy was judged upon his ability to learn and those who were unable to do this did not long remain in the school. The boys were fed, clothed and maintained by the Abbey in the charge of the Almoner. The school existed to provide singing boys for the services in Church and to provide candidates for minor offices in the clergy and later to take the course of ordination for the Priesthood. The objectives of the school involved the teaching of Latin in which all the Church services and the books in the library were written. The boys, therefore, were taught to read, write and speak Latin as the basis for their advancement into the ranks of the clergy or perhaps into the select company of the professed brethren of the Abbey.

The Novices were rarely more than 3 or 4 at any one time and some came

The school for boys

from the Abbey School but they were mainly older men from other walks of life. The minimum age of acceptance was 17. The Candidate usually stayed a few days in the Guest House and was expected to confess his whole life to the Abbot who required to know the most intimate details about his parentage. If he was illegitimate a dispensation would have to be secured before his acceptance. The Candidate's state of health was enquired into to discover if he had a secret malady, if he was good tempered and whether he consorted with women. The Candidate was then received by the Abbot in full Chapter and informed of the disciplines of the Order – perpetual chastity, poverty and obedience. After the Chapter had received the Candidate and if his examination had been satisfactory, he was shaved and re-clothed in a novice's garments and then brought before the morning Chapter again and asked if he was prepared for the kind of life before him. He was then granted a year's probation and placed in the custody of the Master of the Novices who was an important officer who had to be 'a person fitted for winning souls'. The Master was expected to be able to sort out any novice who felt a call to a higher life and one who may regard it as a passing whim. For twelve months the Master and Novice were constant companions day and night. In Frater, Dortor and Church special places were reserved for novices under the watchful eye of the Master, otherwise they were kept apart from the brethren. The Novice had quite a lot to learn in twelve months and instruction was given morning and afternoon, usually in the western cloister alley which became the schoolroom. Each lesson commenced with all reciting *De Profundis* and a prayer. The newcomer first had lessons in the proper way to wear a monk's habit and cowl; how to walk with modesty and gravity; how to bow correctly; to get into bed with due modesty and rise from bed correctly. In short to learn correct behaviour and the manners and customs of the monastic life. This was followed in due course with prayers and psalms which had to be learnt by heart and singing, chanting and reading for which the Latin language was taught. Difficult though this may have been the Master was always at hand to help and encourage.

The behaviour of the novices in the Frater was also of some importance. Eating meals with dirty hands was unforgivable. They should be washed before meals at the lavatory outside the frater doorway and the knife allocated to the novice must be kept sharp and clean. He was also taught to say grace and was sometimes directed by the Master to say grace at the High Table after meals. He was not to seize upon the vegetables, nor use his own spoon in the common dish. He was not to lean upon the table, cut or dirty table-cloths, nor must he use his knife to carry gravy to his mouth nor help others from the dishes as only the ill-mannered and clowns take everything for themselves. Before cutting the common cheese he must wipe his knife and he must not taste the cheese first to see if it was palatable. When the meal ended the knife must be cleaned and covered over with his napkin and left in his place at table. Such elementary instruction may seem superfluous to us today but in those times good manners and decorum was rarely seen outside the precincts of monastic houses.

The lighting of the candles in Church before Matins and other services and the distribution of the graduals and psalters was among the duties undertaken by the novices.

During the probationary period, if he had a desire to continue, the Master brough the Novice before the morning Chapter and in the centre of the House he knelt in the midst of the brethren and begged to be received into the Order. This occurred three times and on the last occasion which was the end of his probation, and when he had retired from the Chapter, the Master was asked for his opinion and the brethren then voted for acceptance or rejection. If it was rejection the novice was forthwith reclothed in worldly attire and left the Abbey. If the decision was favourable, a day was decided upon when the novice should take his vows in Chapter. An occasion of great solemnity, the vows being taken, each brother gave the novice a kiss of peace as a token of acceptance. Dressed in a Monk's habit, the hood was fastened over his head and remained there for three days in token of our Lord's burial in the tomb and his rising again on the third day, and on the third day at morning Mass in Church the Abbot or Prior with some ceremony unfastened the hood and the Novice entered a new life as a junior Monk, but for some years after he was still watched over by the Master of the Juniors.

A young Monk of outstanding intelligence and on the recommendation of the Master could be sent to Oxford to take a degree course in Divinity at Rewley House founded in 1272 or to St. Bernard's College founded in 1437, the Abbey undertaking to meet the expense and maintain their candidate for Holy Orders for several years subject to good reports.

There were also lay novices in the early period for entry into the ranks of the conversi. These recruits came in part from boys in the Abbey School who could not or would not learn or who had preference for the conversi life which in the early period attracted men from all walks of life but later became the refuge of poor men threatened by starvation.

The average life of the professed monk was 55 years. He had no possessions and everything was provided for him. His time was spent in innumerable services, study, silence and in the early period heavy manual labour in the fields which in later times was confined to harvest times. His home was the cloister where he was surrounded by all the buildings and places to which he would be called by routine or duty. He never needed to go beyond the cloister in later times and he was shut away from the world and all excitement. His devotions and duties were ruled by the natural day and natural night. There were indeed no clocks so that long days and short nights (summer) and short days and long nights (winter) determined the time and length of most offices in Church, frater, dortor and Chapter House. He was expected to take Holy Communion every Sunday and on Xmas day, Maundy Thursday, Easter day and Whitsun day. He attended the Chapter House daily where the affairs of the community were decided and on work-days he did various kinds of manual labour which became less and less of a priority as time passed. On Sundays and non-manual labour days, more time was absorbed in reading and study and visits to the gardens and cemetery. Certain duties like serving in the kitchen and frater were shared on a rota basis.

Diet consisted of a snack after Prime at daybreak known as mixtum, consisting of 4 oz. (114 gr.) of bread and one third of a pint (2 dl) of wine or beer. One main meal, dinner, was taken at about 11–15 am or 12–15 pm on a working day and this consisted of two courses, and at about 6 pm of one dish with a plate of cheese or nuts was taken for supper. Fast days cut down even these frugal meals to one a day and the precise time that meals were taken depended upon the seasons of the year. No meat was eaten unless the brother was sick and then it had to be eaten in the Infirmary or the misericord (a room set aside for the purpose). His daily ration of bread was one pound in weight (454 gr.) In the earlier period the diet was low and indigestion prevalent, while periodic blood-letting was the medieval remedy for most sicknesses of the body and this in turn was a weakening experience. It was undoubtedly a hard life in the earlier centuries, especially in winter when there was no heat except in the common room. Called from his cold sleeping-place in the dortor soon after

Monks at work: the holy-water clerk; in the fields; the tabula (struck three times to assemble the brethren); Thursday.

midnight he went into a freezing Church and was expected to sing and pray with fervour for about two hours. Altogether the routine of monastic life could become monotonous and wearisome, sickness being the only release from routine and duties. The Obedientaries had a more interesting life, but having regard to the poverty, insecurity and cruelty in the world outside there were worthwhile compensations in the ordered life of the Cloister which later became pleasant and congenial.

In an enclosed community of some 80 men or more in its heyday there were some odd individuals who would not conform to routine and discipline. Punishment took the form of a penance which was gladly accepted as atonement for any wrong-doing, but for serious crime there was a prison where punishment could be severe. Absconding from an Abbey was regarded as serious and the only evidence we have of such a case is that recorded in the Patent Rolls of Edward 111 Bk. 59. M6d, which reads as follows:

Appointment of John Doubermann and John Cary, clerk, to arrest wherever found Brother John de Pernyle, monk of the monastery of Donkeswylle of the Cistercian Order, who has spurned the habit of his Order and is now a vagabond in secular attire, and deliver him to his Abbot to be chastised according to the rule of the Order (9–12–1346.)

What the fate of Brother John de Pernyle was we shall never know.

The conversi were also Monks and they played an important part in the daily life. Their manual labour in the fields and their crafts within the precinct provided the basis upon which the Abbey functioned and developed. They had their own Prior, frater and dortor and Chapter in the early period and attended all services in Church when their duties allowed except Matins which they were excused. They did not become Obedientaries but they had charge of Abbey Granges and farms and some other services under the direction of the Cellarer. For 150 years they maintained a separate identity in the community but over the years their numbers gradually dwindled away until they finally disappeared with the coming of the Black Death in 1348.

The daily life and routine of the Abbey varied according to the season of the year; whether the day was a working day or a non working day while on Sundays and Fast and other days special arrangements often applied. The following however can be said to be a general pattern of a normal working day.

Matins was the regular night service in Church to which the professed brethren were summoned sometime after midnight from their sleeping-places in the dortor. All wore their night clothes and were out of their beds for nearly two hours.

Prime was the first service of the day at daybreak and when the bell first rang for this it allowed time for day dress and shoes to be put on. When the bell ceased to ring it was the signal to proceed down the night stairs and into the Church. The available conversi assembled in the Nave. The service consisted of a hymn, three psalms and this simple but moving morning prayer:

O Lord God Almighty, who hast brought us to the beginning of this day so assist us by thy grace that we may not fall this day into sin, but that our words may be spoken and our thoughts and deeds directed according to thy just commands.

This service was short and after it the professed brethren went to the water-trough in the south cloister near the frater to wash and complete their dressing for the day, seniors first and juniors last. When all had completed their toilet they proceeded to the frater nearby where a breakfast called 'mixtum' was taken standing up. It was not long before the bell again began to toll for High Mass at about 7 am called mainly for the benefit of the lay people associated with the community. It lasted about one hour. (On non-working days High Mass was substituted by Morning Mass, the High Mass being deferred until 10 am.) At the end of the Mass the bell was kept ringing until the Abbot and the Obedientaries had conferred about matters to bring before the Chapter and when the bell ceased ringing the brethren formed up in procession with the juniors leading the way to the Chapter House. The Abbot was the last in the procession and all stood and bowed to him as he passed through their ranks to reach his chair in the centre of the east wall. The Prior then came forward, and bowed, kissed the Abbot's hand, bowed again and then the Abbot seated himself. This was the signal for all present to seat themselves upon the stone benches around the chamber. A Monk deputed to do so went to the pulpit and read the martyrology for the day and a priest followed and read certain psalms and collects. Another Priest read out the Chapter of the Benedictine rule for the day from which the chamber derived its name and then the obituaries were announced. The list of duties for the following week was read out together with the names of the brethren allocated to do them, when each one rose in his place as his name was called out and bowed. Then a sermon followed which usually was given by the Abbot after which the novices and any conversi present were required to leave the chamber. Afterwards, the first business was the correction of faults. In connection with this matter the 'circator' was a most important person. Appointed to the office by the Abbot, his chief duty seemed to be to circulate around the House and the precinct to see and listen to anything that was going on. If a brother confessed to any misdemeanour the circator would be called upon to inform the Chapter what he had seen and heard about the incident – suspicion was ruled out. A monk who did not confess to a misdemeanour could be accused by another and, likewise, his accusation must be based upon what he actually saw and heard and not on what he suspected. The accused could not make any excuses or in any way defend himself. The Abbot would finally pronounce judgement. It could be a penance such as loss of seniority and taking the last place in the community; strict silence for a period or sitting on the floor of the frater during meals on certain days and being served with bread and water or no meal at all. Another form of punishment was prostration on the floor at the Church door when every monk would have to step over the culprit. The Abbot could prescribe a flogging which must not be done by the accuser but only by an equal or a superior. The accused knelt down in the centre of the Chapter House and stripped to the waist. The person deputed by the Abbot to do the flogging would continue to flog until the Abbot called upon him to desist, when he would assist the victim to rise and put on his clothes. This rather painful experience was regarded as an element of religious devotion and was not resented in any way: the rod and espionage were the two most important pillars of monastic discipline. After the punishment of faults there followed the temporal matters of the Abbey and the affairs of the estate, the admission of novices which was voted upon, the remembrance of departed brethren who, upon their decease, rested for a while in the Chapter House before proceeding on their way to their last resting place. Here, in the 13th. century, the early Abbots were laid to rest in front of the Abbot's chair so that when addressing the community the Abbot could stand upon the burial place of his predecessors and thus receive strength.

When the Chapter meeting ended at about 8.30 am the Tabula in the cloister (a board hit with a malet) was sounded once or twice at intervals. This was the signal for all to assemble in the cloister except those who had already been allocated duties. Manual labour tasks were then allocated by the Prior who, when the necessary tools had been obtained from the Cellarer, led them to the fields, or the down and waste land which they cleared of scrub and undergrowth, ploughed up and cultivated. These were days when the professed worked together with the conversi in joint operations, but in later times the conversi were under the direction of the Cellarer and the professed were assembled on special occasions at hay and corn harvest times when the conversi needed help. Except at harvest-time when they worked on until late in the afternoon, the working-party returned to the precinct sometime after midday, handed in their tools and prepared themselves for a meal.

The Frater, and the kitchen

Upon entering the Frater in processional order they went to their seats and stood at table until the Abbot or his deputy entered when he was bowed to as he made his way to the High Table. The Abbot then gave the signal for grace to be chanted after which the reader for the day came to the centre of the chamber to receive the blessing and then proceed to the pulpit when all around sat down upon their seats. When ready the Abbot rang a small bell called the scylla and the reading commenced. The servers brought the meals to table from the hatch in the west wall where it was brought by two servers in the kitchen. At a signal from the High Table the second course was set upon the tables but before it was eaten, if a brother had died the Almoner brought into the Frater the poor man selected for that day to receive the meal of the departed Monk which had been placed before his vacant chair at table and in front of the cross which stood to mark the place. A server packed up the meal which the poor man took away to eat elsewhere, after which the second course was proceeded with. This was done for 30 days in remembrance of the dead Monk. Silence was enforced throughout the meal to listen to the reader in the pulpit who usually read from a book about the life of a saint or other suitable subject. The meal was usually of two courses, plentiful and good, with a variety of dishes from which to make a choice, the menu including fish from the Abbey fishponds, vegetables from the Abbey gardens as well as fruit, pastry, cheese, wine, water and milk. Beer was commonly drunk (there was no tea, coffee or cocoa).

When the meal had come to an end the Abbot gave a signal and two juniors with baskets came to the centre of the frater and, bowing to the Abbot, proceeded to collect from the table any food not eaten and this was given to the poor in the Almonry. When the left-overs had been collected the Abbot rang the scylla bell and all rose in their places when the reader in the pulpit led the chanting of grace. Sometimes a Novice was deputed to go to the High Table and say grace. Then the brethren filed out of the Frater, the Abbot or the Presiding Officer leading the way.

After dinner in summer it was usual for the brethren to take an hour's rest in the dorter. This was followed by the service of Nones at 3 pm in the Church and then a period of about two or three hours was used for reading and study in the north Cloister alley, for walking or working in the gardens and cemetery or for a quiet game of bowls upon the greensward outside the claustral buildings.

At about 5 pm in summer the brethren re-assembled when the bell tolled for Vespers or Evensong. This was about an hour's service after which supper was taken in the frater which consisted of one full dish and a plate of cheese or nuts.

In the interval before nightfall Collation was a brief period when the Abbot or Senior brother read aloud in the north cloister alley a passage from the bible or other book. Then there followed a short interval after Collation for a walk in the cloister or a warm up in the Common room – the only place in the winter months where a fire was kept burning for the general use of the brethren.

At nightfall the bell rang for the last service of the day – Compline. It took place at about 8 pm in summer and lasted about 30 minutes. It was a service of song and at the end, in silent procession, the brethren filed out of the Church, each one on leaving being sprayed with Holy Water as they made their way to the dorter for sleep at about 8.30 p.m. (earlier in winter).

We have described the routine on a working day but there was a routine for non-working days which was somewhat different. The 7 am High Mass was changed to Morning Mass which allowed the Chapter to meet at about 8 am and at the conclusion of the Chapter meeting the brethren were free to gather in the cloister for discussion and conversation on matters of community interest. The Abbot and the Obedientaries were usually available to discuss any matter with brethren. In the cloister were a number of groups discussing different matters and a brother could attach himself to any group and listen or take part, but the rule warned him to watch his tongue, not to signal to another brother in another part of the cloister and to observe modesty and moderation. This free discussion was known as the 'parliament' from which the secular institution adopted its name. The Parliament came to an end when the bell rang for Tierce at 9 am.

It was not long after the service of Tierce when the first bell for High Mass at 10 am began to toll. The first bell was a signal for all the brethren who were not scheduled for duties to assemble in the cloister and form themselves into processional form – juniors in front and seniors in the rear. After an interval of

In the cloister, quire service, acolytes

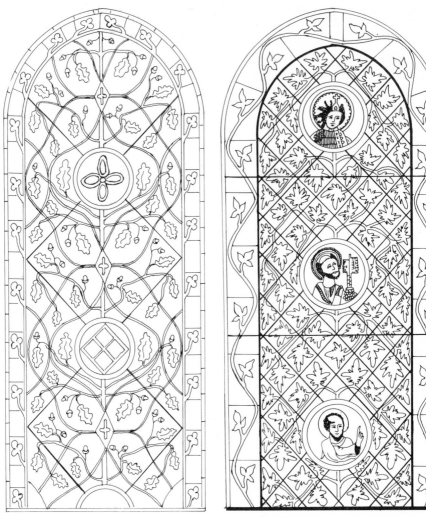

Thirteenth-century 'grisaille' window

Thirteenth/fourteenth-century window — top, St Michael, middle, St Peter, bottom, St John (both based on Simcoe sketches of c. 1840)

silence the second bell tolled softly and slowly and without haste the procession wound its way into Church where each of the brethren took their places – the available conversi assembled at the same time in the nave.

On Sundays and certain other days special arrangements were made for High Mass and the Processionals. On these occasions the community assembled in the cloister at the tolling of the bell and at 10 am entered the Church. Then followed a detailed and complex proceeding. The exorcism and the blessing of the salt and water in Church was followed by the blessed salt being taken to the Fraterer whose duty it was to see that a small quantity of it was placed in every salt cellar in the frater and when each individual there had been sprinkled with Holy Water it was taken back into Church and sprinkled over each person there. The Holy Water was then taken around the House by two Priests and two brethren who between them sprinkled every public room and chamber, the dorter and beds of the lay and professed brethren, the Infirmary and each individual there. In the meantime the altars in Church were sprinkled with Holy Water and under the direction of the Precentor the community passed in procession into the Cloister. First came the Holy Water bearer, next came the cross with an acolyte carrying a lighted candle on each side of the bearer. Behind them came the sub-deacon with the Gospels and following him was the Priest who was to celebrate Mass with his deacon beside him. Then followed two-by-two in double lines about four feet behind each other the whole of the professed brethren with the Abbot walking alone at the end of the procession. They slowly walked around the cloister singing and then went to the west door of the Church where the procession reformed and proceeded into the Nave with the Abbot at the head. Before the Nave altar the Abbot stood with the professed brethren standing behind him in two rows stretching back towards the west door of the Church with the conversi standing on each side. The Nave was sprinkled with Holy Water and also any Chapels around it, after which the procession moved through the centre door of the pulpitum and into the Choir of the Lady Chapel when the main service of High

A Processional; the abbot in the rear as he appears on the Lincumb charter seal of 1235 – 49

Mass took place. On penitential days, on Wednesday and Friday in Lent and on Rogation days, they did this processional on bare feet.

On Easter day, Ascension day, Pentecost and the Assumption of the Blessed Virgin the great processionals were arranged when the cemetery was a station on the route where a pause was made to remember departed brethren, and then on to the Infirmary to visit the sick. The processionals were regarded as important diversions from the monotony of the regular routine and they were looked forward to by the community.

Dunkeswell Abbey: reconstructed from the sketch made in 1794 by the Rev. John Swete; location, west of the Conventual Church. Note the tower on the left standing at the north-west corner of the nave of the church, as seen by the artist; believed to be the Infirmary with the Infirmerer's lodge adjoining (Devon Record Office D564, vol. 9)

The Infirmary occupied an important part in the life of the community. It contained a large Hall with at least one aisle and probably two, in each of which couch beds were placed with their heads to the wall leaving an open space in the centre in which an open fire burned, the smoke finding its way out through a hole or form of chimney in the roof. Near the Hall was the Infirmarer's lodging and another part was reserved for the aged and infirm who, after 50 years of the professed life, were considered entitled to take up their abode in the Infirmary where the rigours of the rule were relaxed. The Master of the Farmery (the Infirmarer) lived on the premises and his duties were laid down. He was enjoined to be affectionate and gentle to those in his charge and give them every consideration. If they could not attend the Infirmary Chapel he must go to their bedside and use words of consolation, but he must not disturb his patients if they were resting. Disease was treated by baths and herbs grown in the Abbey physic garden – the complaints and diseases included fever, toothache, gout, affections of the brain, eyes, throat, spleen, liver, body pains and sudden illness. Medieval medical knowledge advocated regular bleedings to keep the body in good health and this was a special feature of the service provided by the Infirmary. It is highly likely that this treatment finished off some of the sick but the Monks were regularly bled to keep them in a good state of health or so they believed. Usually in Chapter, four times a year, the Abbot selected the brethren he wished to be bled. The operation was done in the common room by the Infirmarer between 9 am and noon over four days and in batches of two to six at a time, the Abbot or his deputy deciding the day of attendance for each individual. The victim could fortify himself against the ordeal beforehand if he wished by going to the frater to eat and drink. Blood was taken from his arm, a styptic applied and the arm bandaged. After this, discipline was relaxed for three days and duties excused except for Matins when they were called up just after midnight to spend an hour-and-a-half in the cold Church. The victim was usually allowed to spend his convalescence in the Infirmary if he wished to do so, where his first meal after the bloodletting was sage and parsley washed down in salt water and a dish of soft eggs followed later by meat. This was a luxury. The Obedientaries did not escape the ordeal and they had to arrange their duties to be covered while they were convalescing after the operation. The Abbot undoubtedly shared this experience with his flock in early times when he lived very close to them, but when he withdrew to apartments of his own in later years he most likely escaped the ordeal. Any brethren unwell from the strain of silence and the sheer monotony of life in the cloister was given duties outside in the garden and open air which involved exercise. In cases of sudden illness the Abbot went to the Infirmary to see the brother so suddenly struck down to enquire about the health of his soul and the purity of his conscience and confirm him in the eternal way of life. In such cases all discipline was relaxed and the Infirmarer exhorted to provide a lamp to burn beside him all night.

When a Monk died the practice adopted by the Orders and individual Monasteries varied in their detail but in the early period the tabula (a board suspended from the wall in the cloister) was struck three times in rapid succession when a Monk was nearing his end. This was the signal for the community to assemble at once and leave whatever they were doing and to proceed in procession singing psalms to the place where the dying Monk was. A portable altar was brought to the bedside and with the community around him, the Abbot or Senior Priest administered the last sacrament. A cross of ashes was sprinkled on a bed or on the floor and over it was laid a sheet of sackcloth. Upon this, in his last breath, the dying Monk was gently placed. When he had expired his body was covered by a quilt and here he remained for some time. Later his body was taken to be washed and wrapped in a winding sheet. In the meantime the community had assembled in the Chapter House where prayers were said and psalms sung until the body was brought to them. If the burial was to take place the next day the dead monk was left in the Chapter House over night and on the next morning it was taken in procession into the Church when the Abbot or Senior Priest sprinkled the body with Holy Water and censed it while the professed sang. After Mass was said, slowly and in procession with the Abbot or the Prior leading, they took the dead monk to the cemetery where, in the presence of the whole community he was laid in the grave and over it a small cross was placed. The departed brother was daily remembered in Church, Chapter and Frater for 30 days after which on the anniversary of his death his name was read out in Chapter. Neighbouring religious houses were advised of his demise and his name was read out in their Chapter. After a lapse of some 12 years or more his bones were recovered from the soil and placed in a charnel house or crypt. The cemetery therefore was only a temporary repository and usually did not occupy much ground near the door of the north Transept of the Church.

In medieval times the Feudal gentry sought an association with a religious house as a benefactor so that in return for their benefactions they would be assured of spiritual benefits after death in the form of a candle burning night and day before the altar of the Conventual Church or the saying of prayers for their souls at certain times of the year. Memorials of this kind to the departed were highly valued at this time.

In the early period when manual labour was a religious obligation of prime importance the canonical offices were rationalised to provide for it but as manual labour receded in importance and became a smaller and subordinate obligation the canonical offices grew in ceremonial and elaboration as more time was devoted to liturgical services, reading and prayer. The Cistercian horarium or daily routine was changed about three times a year to correspond with winter, lenten and summer. Winter began on 13 September and continued until Ash Wednesday – the first day of Lent. This was followed by 40 days of fasting and after Easter the summer began and ended on 12 September.

The Abbey was not only a place where prayers were said but where people ate and drank, wore out shoes and clothes, cared for the sick, fed the old and the hungry, and entertained guests – many of whom were pilgrims humble and of rank, minstrels, merchants, pedlars, nobles and others – all of whom were treated as befitted their status.

Wool and linen for clothes was spun and woven from their own sheep's wool, cut out and made in the cloistral buildings. Skins of their own cattle were cured and tanned on the spot to provide leather for making into boots and shoes which were also made in the precinct. Vegetables and fruit were supplied by the convent gardens, fish from the fishponds and their own grain from their own fields was ground in their own mills to provide flour and malt for bread and beer to feed the residents in the Abbey precinct, including a fair number of lay servants. Bees were kept for their honey, doves and poultry and pigeons bred for the table. There were carpenters, masons, blacksmiths, bakers etc. All these activities and more had to be organised by the Abbot and his Obedientaries so that life was anything but dull for the professed monks who took part in them. For those who chose to withdraw from external activity life could become monotonous unless they were academically inclined.

A Cistercian monastery although geographically isolated was nevertheless a world of its own in which each individual made his own contribution to a communal way of life designed to provide a self-sufficient community independent of the world outside its boundaries. The ordered life within the precinct, the clean and well furnished accommodation with meals at regular intervals properly cooked and generously served in an atmosphere of good manners and decency, contrasted sharply with the rough and raw nature of life in the world outside with its vices, improvidence and irresponsibilities. It was an education in itself to be a Guest of the Abbey which made a profound impression upon the feudal nobility and their associates, whose manners and conduct was often atrocious on their own estates.

CHAPTER SIX

The Abbey and the Church

The Abbey and the Church: Wulferchurche. The Church in Parish life. The Impropriated Churches – Dunkeswell, Sheldon – Dotton – Auliscombe. The Church and Church-yard often the site of fairs and markets. The Vicars – tythe. Abbey 'Titles' for the Priesthood. Monks ordained. Convocation of the Clergy.

THROUGHOUT its existence the Abbey had a close association with the Church and the Diocesan Authorities. Despite the fact that Cistercian Abbeys were exempted from the Bishop's visitation, he did nevertheless have great influence over the conduct and behaviour of the brethren who resided in the Abbey and could for reasons of his own excommunicate a monk or even interdict any House for outrageous and disorderly conduct.

At the time of its foundation in 1201 the founder gave Wulferchurche to the Abbey. It was a small Church in the Manor of Dunkeswell which had come down from Saxon times. It took its name from King Wulfer of the Mercians (657–675), who was the first Mercian King to embrace Christianity. Aethelbald, who succeeded to the Crown of Mercia, invaded Devon in 743 from the north in support of the West Saxons of whom he was the overlord, and whose boundaries with neighbouring Dumnonia were along the crest of the ridge of the nearby Blackdown Hills. At the extremity of his advance he dedicated churches to the memory of persons known to him for their Christian piety and here he dedicated the church to the memory of King Wulfer. The church was serviced and maintained by Dunkeswell Abbey during the 338 years it was in their possession, but after the dissolution in 1539 there was no authority responsible for its care and maintenance and the church fell into ruins; it was rebuilt in 1801 by the late Lt. General John Graves Simcoe who had been the first Lieutenant-Governor of Upper Canada (now Ontario) in the years 1792–96. He lies buried in the precinct of what is now called Wolford Chapel.

Some 40 years after its foundation four Parish Churches were appropriated to the Abbey by the Bishop of Exeter, William Brewer, nephew of the founder. They were located at Dunkeswell, Sheldon, Auliscombe and at Dotton near

(Wulgerchurche) Wolford Chapel as rebuilt in 1801.

The Chapel stands on the ancient precincts of a former Church, & over the Bones of those who have departed centuries ago.

Based on a sketch by John Graves Simcoe, 19 August 1801

Collaton Raleigh, some 18 miles south west of the Abbey. The reasons given by the Bishop for doing this were 'the daily hospitality exercised by the monks and the increase of their means of exercising their benevolence'.

Churches were in a very bad state of repair in this interim period between the timber-constructed Saxon churches and the Norman stone-built church introduced after 1066. The stone-built church was more expensive to construct and the financial resources of the Abbeys were sought by transferring to their custody churches situated in areas where the Abbey had substantial land holdings. Later on, however, particularly in the 15th. century, this practice was abused by some Abbeys seeking and obtaining from the Bishop appropriations of Parish Churches as a means of augmenting their revenues. The stone-built church in the early period often had a thatched roof and earthen floors over which were strewn rushes and straw which was renewed two or three times a year. Around the walls were low seats or benches upon which the weaker members of the congregation were allowed by custom to sit during the long services, while the fit and well remained standing throughout. 'The weakest to the wall' aptly described the scene at church services, where, before their eyes, painted high upon the wall above the Chancel arch was the scene of the Crucifixion or the Last Judgement.

The church was the place where parishioners were baptised, married and buried and it was the centre of social life for the people who lived in a geographical area called the Parish – a unit of ecclesiastical administration whose influence upon the life of the people was as great if not greater than that of the Lord of the Manor. Fairs and markets were sometimes held in the church and the churchyard and this was so at Dotton as late as the year 1400. There were religious festivals at Easter and Christmas and the harvest festival in September, as well as the May Day and the Midsummer Day festivals, in all of which the church was involved. The open land immediately around the church was the 'coemeterium', meaning the dormitory or sleeping-place of the dead. Animals grazed over it and it often was the site of the local market and fair. In 1267 Bishop Quevil of Exeter directed that a wall should be built to securely enclose the cemetery and that no animal or pasturage be permitted upon it. Trees were to be encouraged to grow around the Church as a windbreak and stone crosses or crucifixes were to be set up as a testimony to the

Parish church of St Nicholas, Dunkeswell, 1794 (Devon Record Office, D.564, vol.9)

Parish church of St James, Sheldon. The tower has a fifteenth-century window and below it the west doorway which at some time was blocked up.

faith and hope of the dead for resurrection. Despite the Bishop's efforts to sanctify the burial-place it was a long time before his directions were fully observed.

The acquisition of the four Parish Churches placed upon the Abbey new responsibilities as well as demands upon its financial resources. The Vicars or Chaplains who serviced these Churches were nominated by the Abbey for the Bishop's approval.

The Parish Church of St. Nicholas at Dunkeswell was completely rebuilt by the Abbey and dedicated by Bishop Bronescombe on the 5 December 1259, and the same Bishop on 20 October 1261 decreed that the Abbey must pay the vicar of the church a stipend of 5½ marks (£3.67p) a year and allow him all special legacies, corn dues and offerings on the greater Festivals. The first vicar we know of is one Thomas, 'parson of Donkeswille', who with Abbot William of 'Donkeswille' witnessed a deed at Canonsleigh Abbey sometime before 1219.

The Parish Church of St. James the Greater at Sheldon came into the possession of Dunkeswell Abbey in 1243, when Bishop William Brewer gave it the church at 'Schildon' together with all its possessions 'to possess freely for their own use forever'. The Abbey undoubtedly rebuilt the Church sometime after 1259 when the church at Dunkeswell was rebuilt. The tower of the church is most probably of the 13th. century, when the Church was entered through a doorway in the west front of the tower which at a later period was blocked up and a south entry provided into the nave. The first known Vicar was Richard who, we are told by Abbot Ralph (1249–51), held a tenement of Dunkeswell Abbey for which he paid a rent of 10p yearly. The vicars of most churches at this time were farmers whose livelihood depended in part upon their farming activities, but in 1269 the Bishop endowed the Vicarage with 5 marks (£3.33p) which meant that the Abbey was charged to pay this annual stipend to the vicar with a part of the tythes received by the Church.

Shortly after the Abbey had acquired the church at Sheldon it also acquired a substantial acreage of woodland, moor and waste-land from the Hospitallers of the Order of St. John of Jerusalem, who had a Priory at nearby Bodmescombe. With this and other waste-land in their possession they assarted and converted much of it into ploughland and meadow. Over a period of many years the Abbey added substantially to the area of cultivated land in the Parish and created an agricultural community of some size with its Manor Court near to the Church, a Grange farm and other lesser farm tenements. The steady growth of the community and its population was reflected in the improvements made to the church in the early years of the 15th century. Then the Abbot, John Bokeland, commissioned Robert Norton of Exeter to cast a new bell, which weighed about 5 cwt (250 kg), for the church about the year 1430. It now stands on the floor of the church. A little later a similar bell was put into the tower and in the West front a 15th.-century window was placed. It is probable the West door into the church was blocked up at this time to strengthen the tower against additional pressures from the heavier bells and a larger window. The nave and the chancel were probably enlarged and extended at this time to provide for a south-door entry into the Church and the installation of backless bench-seating.

After the Black Death in 1348 the church was serviced by the Abbey Priests; that is to say that monks, ordained priests for the service of the Abbey Church, were made available to service the impropriated churches of the Abbey of which Sheldon was one. This practice continued down to the dissolution in 1539 when in the deed of surrender of the Abbey the monk John Gaye was appointed to the 'cure' of Sheldon at a stipend of £6.67p a year and Abbot John Ley was appointed Rector of Sheldon and Sainthill. On 27 May 1557 John Ley went to Payhembury as vicar and died there a few years later.

The Parish Church at Awliscombe was appropriated to Dunkeswell Abbey by the Bishop of Exeter, William Brewer, probably at the time the other churches were transferred. The Abbot of Dunkeswell in 1291 declared the income of the Rectory to be £10 and the Abbey had the right to nominate the

Tower of the Parish church of St Michael & All Angels, Awliscombe (formerly St Margarets Church – 14th/15th century)

vicars for the Bishop's approval. It is recorded, however, that in the closing months of the great plague in 1348 the Abbey failed to nominate a candidate for the vacancy undoubtedly caused by the death of the incumbent and the failure of the Abbey to nominate a successor reflects a state of confusion at Dunkeswell Abbey, which did not escape the ravages of the Black Death at this time. In February 1349 the Bishop stepped in and instituted a young priest named Robert Marachal who remained the vicar of Awliscombe for 44 years, retiring in 1393.

There is little doubt that the Abbey rebuilt the church at Awliscombe sometime in the 13th. or 14th. century. Standing on high ground, the church presents a magnificent appearance on its western frontage. As at Sheldon, the tower contained a bell cast in the 15th. century, which now stands on the floor of the church and bears the inscription 'Sancta Margaretta Ova Pro Novis', which roughly translated means 'To the glory of St. Margaret', so we can deduce that the church in the 15th. century was dedicated to St. Margaret. The earliest vicar we know of is the William de Quenton who, as we have seen, in the year 1327 broke into the enclosed premises of the Prior of the Hospitallers at Bodmescombe in an aggressive mood, and armed.

The fifth church to belong to Dunkeswell Abbey was the small church of St. David of Dotton (Collaton Raleigh). It was appropriated to the Abbey by Bishop William Brewer on 30 September 1242. Some years later it was visited by Bishop Bronescombe, who writes in folio 11 of his Register dated 5

February 1259 that he discovered the monks had closed the church, sent away the parishioners and prevented them from cultivating the land. The monks were ordered by the Bishop to restore the church and provide for divine worship, and to restore all lands, rights and privileges of the parishioners. This they agreed to do and kept their promise to Bishop Bronescombe for nearly 300 years until the dissolution in 1539, when the church was known as the Church of St. Mary at Dotton.

The church being some 18 miles distant from the Abbey and in the Deanery of Aylesbeare, the Abbots had to make arrangements for it to be serviced by a local parson. In July 1400 Bishop Stafford addressed a Commission to the Dean of Aylesbeare and to the Vicar of Otterton (Walter Caprugg) who served the Church for the Abbey. After mentioning that Christ himself had set an example by driving out the buyers and sellers whose trading had changed the Temple from a House of prayer to a den of thieves, the Commission continues:

Many people and often from diverse Parishes, foregather at the Church of the Parish of Dotton and in the Churchyard there, holding a food market, feasting several days and nights, making uproar, not attending divine offices and woefully and unjustly impeding the people of the place from making their prescribed devotions to the great peril of their souls, and other pernicious things. We indeed, not wishing this form of transgression to continue as hitherto, firmly and strongly commit and order you . . . once, twice and a third time, admitting no refusal, to instigate and see it well remembered by one and all, that commercial transactions, food markets, taking of bread and indulgence in drink, and uproar in the said Church and Churchyard, to be wholly ceased, discontinued and desisted from henceforth . . . and not to violate the sanctuaries under pain of greater excommunication . . . if any shall disobey your admonitions . . . you are to cite them to appear before us or our Commissioner in our Cathedral Church of Exeter, 15 lawful days after citation . . . (Stafford Register Vol. 2 fol. 227).

The land of the church was leased to a bailiff of the Abbey in 1532 – William Stoforde, who paid a rent of £1. The church however has long since ceased to exist.

It is of interest to note that the vicars of Churches at this time were forbidden to marry but they could have a 'hearth mate' to look after their domestic affairs. In addition to their slender stipends they received about one half of the Parochial tythes payable to the church and the income from fees received from Baptisms, Marriages, Burials and offerings given in Church services. They received the offerings made at the Churching of women, a custom in which a pregnant woman near to her time of delivery was received at the church door by the vicar or priest, who said 'Come into the Temple of God. Adore the son of the Blessed Virgin Mary who has given thee fruitfulness in childbearing'. The woman knelt before the altar, received the sacrament and was blessed by the priest.

From these resources however the vicar was responsible for the repair of the chancel of the church when necessary; for the provision and renewal of service books and payment of dues to the Bishop and Archdeacon. He was also liable for divine service in the church and to pay for any assistant clerics he might need for his spiritual duties and for alleviating the plight of the poor and sick of his Parish.

In the 13th. century the Parish priest and the local community of the village, rarely exceeding some 60 dwellings, were very close associates. The priest, cut off as he was in most Parishes from contact with the outside world, was a farmer, working very often side by side with his people in the open fields. He often met them at the village mill or the village well and day by day he faced the dangers and disasters which commonly threatened their security and their lives.

To the community the birth of a child in the village was of considerable importance, as great interest was shown in its anticipated birth and post-natal condition. It was of great importance that the child should be baptised on the day of its birth or very soon after, otherwise an unbaptised child had no hope of being received into heaven – and these were days of high infant mortality.

Marriage was regarded as a symbol or a sacrament. Children of a tender age were married off by their parents, especially if they were people who held land and were anxious that a line of succession should be established in order to retain the land within the family. The practice frequently denied the children any choice of their own and young girls were married to old men, boys to widows, children of four or five years of age married off to grown up men and women. The first stage was the 'troth plight' in which, after the parents had come to an agreement, the couple clasped hands, rings were given and received and a declaration of intent to marriage was made. The church ceremony was usually deferred until the bridegroom was sure his bride was capable of bearing children and this custom led to a high proportion of brides being pregnant at the time of the marriage ceremony.

The Bishops commanded the local clergy always to be ready and prepared to visit the sick when summoned and not to be deterred by rain or thunder. The visit of the priest to the sick person was carried out with dignity and reverence. The priest travelled along the country lanes and across open fields with his clerk carrying before him the cross, and a lantern, and ringing a bell. This often was regarded by those who saw it as a preparation for death which excited a condition of superstition and terror in the minds of simple people.

The burial of the dead was carried out by the priest in a solemn and dignified service, and the dead were remembered in the following Sunday service in the Parish Church.

From the cradle to the grave and beyond it the church kept in touch with its members and sought to strengthen and sustain them. Apart from the church there was no other body to whom the people could turn for support and strength to overcome life's problems in a life which was often rough, coarse and brutal.

Tythe was a system of tax paid for centuries by parishioners to the Parish Church. It was a payment of one tenth 'of all fruits and profit justly acquired' and was so wide in its application as to include one tenth of the annual crop of hay, corn, wool, wine etc., and on the natural increase of livestock of all kinds as well as upon milk and cheese, fruits and vegetables, eggs, rabbits, bees with their honey and suchlike. Personal tythe was the payment of one tenth from business and trading activities which included the product of the craftsman, the profit of the miller and the ale seller, the tinker, the tailor and others who paid their tythe to the Parish Church where they were bound by law to receive the sacrament. The system was so wide as to make it impossible to check, especially on the larger Manors, and so there was evasion. To ensure that evasion was kept down to the lowest level the penalty for non-payment of tythe was excommunication from the Church, which was at that time a serious disability for any parishioner. The tythe was divided between the rector and the vicar of the Parish, who shared the responsibility for the maintenance of the structure of the church and its internal services. In the case of the impropriated churches of Dunkeswell Abbey the Abbot had the right to receive all the tythes where the Abbey serviced the church with its own priests: in 1536 these amounts totalled £1.30p from Dotton; £5.26p from Dunkeswell; £3.51 from Sheldon and from Awliscombe which was serviced by a vicar, the Rectorial share of the tythe was £9 from the tythe of sheaves (corn).

The Abbey throughout its existence took an active interest in the recruitment of the Parochial Clergy and over the period 1395–1455 it granted 75 'Titles' to candidates for the various stages of the priesthood, which meant that the Abbey undertook to provide adequate maintainance for candidates seeking ordination until they were placed in benefices. This involved support for ordination as sub-deacon at 18, deacon at 20 and priest at 25 years of age, and continued support should he secure a place at Rewley House or St. Bernard's College at Oxford to study for the D.D. degree. Without a 'Title' a candidate for the Priesthood was not accepted. A fruitful source of candidates for the Priesthood came from the Abbey school.

During the period 1400–55 the Abbots arranged for 32 monks to seek ordination for the stages of the Priesthood for service in the Conventual Church and the impropriated Churches. Among them was John Bokeland in 1400, who became the Abbot in 1419, and Trystram Crukern in 1422 who went to Newenham Abbey and became Abbot there from 1431 to 1456. John Otery was sent for ordination in 1430 and was Abbot of Dunkeswell for the period 1439–69.

The Abbots of Dunkeswell were regular attenders at the Convocation of the

Clergy, the Ecclesiastical Parliament, which met for varying periods of time at St. Paul's in London, where decisions were made upon a variety of subjects, including the rate of taxation to be levied upon Ecclesiastical benefices (which involved of course the rate of taxation to be paid by Monasteries and Religious Houses). The Abbots journeyed too and from St. Paul's on horseback accompanied by a retinue of servants and a knight to protect them, the journey taking three to four days each way.

The Convocations at this time were much concerned among other things with the spread of heresy and how to combat it. From time to time over a long period it also considered the measure of financial support it would give to the King and the Pope in their Crusade campaigns to drive the infidels out of the Holy Land. The Abbots of Dunkeswell therefore had responsibilities for national policies which they helped to shape.

CHAPTER SEVEN

Years of Disaster and Change

Years of Disaster and Change: Loans raised for reconstruction. The Black Death strikes – mortality – effect on Manor life. Change from arable to livestock farming – growth of rented tenancies and wage labour. The Asthorpe affair – unsettled times. The Abbot takes Court action. Suppression of lawlessness. The Cistercian community recovers. Abbot Whitmore and the orphan child. Royal impositions. The Abbot's powers again challenged.

WHEN the famine years of 1315–16 had passed there followed a long period of exceptional prosperity in agriculture, when harvests were bountiful and prices low. This provided a favourable opportunity for the Abbey to undertake work of reconstruction which must have been long overdue. During this period loans totalling at least £1,169 were raised – a very large sum for those times. A loan of £500 from John Gaunt of Berkyng, London, was repaid on 11 October 1347 and a loan of £500 from Henry, Earl of Lancaster (Patron of the Abbey), was repaid on 29 May 1347. The last loan of £89.70p was raised on 9 February 1347 from Robert de Brodeham and William de Todenham of London, mercers. This was undoubtedly for the supply of textile fabrics, furnishings and linen etc., supplied by men in that trade. The fabrics and furnishings would have been required for premises recently reconstructed or improved.

Against this background of prosperity an event occurred that brought disastrous consequences to the Abbey and dramatically changed the whole pattern of social life. It was the Black Death; a name given to a plague which took off almost half the population of the country and swept through Devon in a matter of months, leaving a trail of devastation in its wake. The plague came from the East and first appeared in July 1348 at Weymouth. Melcombe, as Weymouth was then called, was a busy sea-port and ships are believed to have brought the plague over with them; rats and fleas spread this form of cholera far and wide. The disease spread rapidly along rivers and water-courses and from there inland to other parts. The plague was no respecter of persons and the strong and vigorous as well as the weak were struck down and died within about three days of its onset. Those who lived in groups and communities were more vulnerable then those living in isolation, and the highly insanitary living conditions of all classes – among whom the diseases of scurvy and leprosy were endemic – provided ideal breeding conditions for the infection. There were few medical men and they were quite unable to come to grips with the incidence of plague. The west country received the first impact of the pestilence which then passed on to Bristol, the North and to London.

History has buried in silence the full extent of the tragedy which befell the Cistercian community at Dunkeswell. John de Wallis was the Abbot when the Plague struck in 1348 but he was no longer the Abbot in 1353. The benefice of the impropriated Church of Auliscombe fell vacant towards the end of the year 1348 but the Abbey failed to nominate a priest for their church, and by default the Bishop instituted a young priest named Richard Marachel on the 17 February 1349. These slender straws indicate there was a state of confusion in the Abbey at this time or that the Abbacy was vacant. The Bishop also in 1349 instituted new priests for the vacant benefices of Upottery, Luppitt, Coombe Raleigh and Broadhembury, all near neighbours of Dunkeswell Abbey. The Bishop normally appointed annually 36 Priests to vacant benefices, but between January and September 1349 he appointed 345, of which only a few were for benefices in Cornwall where the plague struck the following year and these, the Bishop said, were as many priests as he could find. In the diocese 48.8 per cent of the beneficed clergy died from the plague. In parishes without clergy the dying went to their graves without the consolation of the last sacrament, and in some cases they remained unburied because no one was left alive capable of burying them. The plague was ravaging the villages along the course of the river Exe in November 1348. It was not until 10 September 1440 that we learn of the fate of a small village called Templeton, near Tiverton, when John Palfreyman, aged 72, giving evidence as to the status of Templeton Chapel at the Archdeacon's enquiry of that date said:

... he heard from his father (who had lived there all his life) that at the time of the first great pestilence the servants (of whom he was one) of William Wyngrave then Rector went with a cart to Templeton to bring back the bodies of the dead by night for burial at Witheridge, and at Belbyford, so full was the cart, one body fell off and William atte Hayne was given a penny to go and fetch it next day.

This witness added that sometimes the Templeton people ran with their babies for baptism to a church nearer than Witheridge when their lives were in danger, and this with the Rector's license. (D & C. Rec. Soc. Lacy Reg Vol. 2. p211).

At the Cistercian Abbey of Newenham only the Abbot and two monks survived out of a community of 26, while within the Abbey walls 88 secular persons perished. The community at Dunkeswell Abbey at this time would not have been very different from that at Newenham and it would be surprising if they did not suffer a like fate.

Amid this sea of catastrophe the Cistercians at Dunkeswell did not escape the devastating effect upon its Manors and estates. The buoyant prosperity of recent years was transformed almost overnight into deep depression. Of the strips of ploughland in the open fields of the Manors half were growing weeds and scrub, their cultivators having died or moved away. Much of the land of the free tenants also was in the same condition and few could be found to take the vacant tenancies, although rents were reduced by one half in an effort to maintain the cultivation of the land. If a new tenant could be found he was required to take care of any orphans left by the previous tenant. The free labourers who survived were able to command double wages for their labour and the servile peasantry that were left made a bid for their freedom from the feudal obligation of labour service upon the Lord's desmesne land. They now demanded payment in money for their labour which in effect made them free wage labourers. Others preferred to pay a money-rent for the land they held instead of doing servile labour on the the Lord's desmesne land. Many villeins absconded if these concessions could not be obtained. They were welcomed with open arms by the Lord and bailiffs of other Manors who were desperately in need of labour, and no questions were asked when they arrived to offer their services. In normal times the Lord would have sent the villein back to the Manor from which he came but it was now every Lord for himself in the scramble to maintain the Manor and cultivate the land. For a villein with a family of children it was much more difficult to abscond, but the pressure of events favoured him and it was much easier for him to withdraw from labour service and pay a nominal rent for his holding. These new rents became known as 'quit' rents, that is to say quit of servile labour for the Lord of the Manor. In a later period quit rents became known as 'customary' rents and this indicated the servile origin of the tenancy as distinct from the 'free' rents of the free tenants.

The Grange farms of the Abbey were seriously disorganised. The conversi had gone and the free labourers who worked upon them were thinned out by death. Those who were left were quite inadequate to maintain the Granges. The hay and corn crops rotted in the ground and what could be harvested was probably less than half the normal crop. The livestock were neglected and disease took them off as the cattlemen and shepherds were no longer available to attend them. The hay and corn crops were so reduced as to be quite inadequate to feed the usual number of livestock during the winter. Coupled to this was the dismal picture of unoccupied cottages and farm-buildings with their thatched roofs falling in and in some cases whole villages wiped out and the dwellings collapsed. Manorial mills stood silent from the death of the miller or from the drying up of corn-supplies for milling. In the year 1377 there were only eight monks at Dunkeswell.

The financial effect of the Black Death upon the Abbey Manors and

Granges was serious. Revenues from the sales of corn, wool and livestock substantially declined. The income from free rents fell and the cost of labour rose. There was no return to the old order when the plague had exhausted itself despite the many attempts to that end – with Parliament fixing wages and prices in a vain attempt to restrict the movement of labour. The Black Death had opened the door to freedom for the peasantry and the Manor had to adapt itself to changes in the way it organised the cultivation of the land. The cultivation of strips of land in three or more large open fields was making way for the enclosure of land by fences and ditches and leasing it to 'customary' and free tenants for money rents. The leases issued for these tenancies were for the life of the tenant, his wife and children, and the free tenant usually held the land for a period of years and sometimes for the life of himself and his family. The shortage of labour, however, continued for many years and this compelled the Lords of the Manors to phase out arable cultivation with its ploughing, sowing, reaping and harvesting and to develop the less labour-intensive activity of sheep-farming, for which purpose arable land was now being grassed down and the pasture and waste-land of the Manor used for intensive sheep- and cattle-farming; for the Lord the shepherd became more important than the ploughman. This change often conflicted with the rights of the Manor tenants who still claimed their entitlement to the use of the pasture and waste-land of the Manor for the grazing of their own cattle and sheep.

The Abbey, therefore, under the management of their stewards and bailiffs developed large-scale sheep- and cattle-farming on the Granges and the desmesne lands of its Manors. The Manor Court, however, continued to function although it had lost for ever that rigid control of the lives and behaviour of the people who lived within its boundary. Nevertheless, it was at the Manor Court that the free and 'customary' tenants paid their rents on certain stipulated dates and here the rules of good husbandry were still enforced under the vigilant eye of the steward or bailiff, and all who lived within its boundary were still obliged to attend its meetings unless exempted. The Manor Court remained down to the dissolution in 1539 and beyond an important unit of local government, but the unsettled conditions following the Black Death undermined its ability to maintain the same degree of discipline in the community in the face of the widespread disorder which continued well into the 15th. century.

One day in the summer of 1384 Sir William Asthorpe, Lord of the Manor of Hemyock, mounted his horse and with two of his servants, William Caresford and Richard Carpenter, went to his fee at Bolham and Bywode to collect the customs and services which he said was due to him from the Abbey at Dunkeswell. Being unable to collect them, Sir William ordered his two servants to round up the cattle of the Abbey on the Manor there and drive them off to

Kynwardleigh, where they were impounded pending a settlement of the matter. A short time afterwards Abbot Robert mustered a small army of men from far and wide consisting of parsons, butchers, tailors, bailiffs, tenants and others, – about 50 all told – and with the Abbot at their head they descended upon the pound at Knywardleigh, broke into it, rescued the cattle, assaulted the servants of Sir William Asthorpe and drove the cattle back to the Abbey. On 25 July 1384, Sir William Asthorpe having complained to the King, a commission was directed by Henry IV to the Judges of Assize to hear the case and report, but nothing seems to have come of it.

The Asthorpe incident was a reflection upon the unsettled conditions of that time when law and order had broken down. Indeed the last half of the 14th. and much of the 15th. century was a long and unsettled period punctuated by famine and pestilence. The plague returned in 1361 and in 1369 and although these subsequent attacks were not so serious as the first onslaught in 1348/9 yet they brought death and destruction in their train and prevented the increase in population so badly needed to replace the mortality of those years. The picture over this long period was one of falling rents and rising labour-costs; land falling out of cultivation and returning again to pasture and waste, while dilapidated farm buildings and cottages continued to fall down and a supreme effort was made to overcome financial insolvency. The Abbots resorted to the Courts to recover debts owing to the Abbey, to prevent trespass, and to claim for damages from the cutting down and carrying away of trees and undergrowth and the destruction of corn and other crops. Long periods of time elapsed, however, between one Court meeting and the next and when it did meet the Court was often unable to deal with the heavy list of cases in one sitting and so the process through the local Courts was very slow. Often the defendants had nothing and could not pay; some could not be found to answer the charges, while others were distrained of all they possessed and forced to leave their land.

The cases taken to Court by the Abbot for debt and trespass were symptoms of a scene of disorder in the countryside. On 22 August 1434 the King appointed the Bishop of Exeter and two Knights of the Shire as Commissioners with powers to summon before them persons of quality, Mayors and Bailiffs to swear on oath not to cherish or take into their service robbers, oppressors of the people, manslayers, felons, outlaws, ravishers of women against the law and unlawful hunters of forests, parks and warrens. The Mayors and Bailiffs were required also to swear their own citizens and burgesses to keep this oath. A few years later the King Commissioned three Knights of the Shire, one of whom was Sir John Dynham (Lord of the Manor of Hemyock), to call together all lieges of the King in Somerset, Dorset, Devon and Cornwall to march against rebels who have 'gathered together in diverse counties of the Realm and propose to subvert the King's estate and the Government of the Realm and destroy the faithful subjects of the King and appropriate their goods.' The Commissioners were to arrest and punish the rebels. It appears the rebels had gathered at Tiverton, and at the request of the Commissioners the Bishop of Exeter on 24 February 1452 sent a letter to John Copplestone warning him 'as one of the Bishop's tenants, to take no part in gatherings against the King, his proclamations or his laws and urging that those already at Tiverton do return home speedily for fear of bloodshed'. (D. & C. Rec. S. Lacy Reg. Vol. 1. pp. 273/4).

The troublous times with its vagrancy, vagabondage and violence, led men of intellect to look to the cloister for fulfilment of their ideals. The Abbey could offer peace, a life of religious devotion, and opportunities for reading and study. The Cistercian community at Dunkeswell grew stronger day by day and their numbers increased from the eight in 1377 to something over 20 in the last century of its existence. Life in the Abbey had changed and the comforts of the body were more in evidence than in earlier times. The dortor was no longer an open draughty chamber with straw mattresses on the floor to sleep on. It had been divided by wainscoting to provide a separate bed-chamber for each brother, with privacy and a low couch to sleep upon. The north-cloister alley was now partitioned to provide private rooms or cells for reading and study and there was more heat available in the winter months. The community was now an intimate and closely knit group of men living together for a common purpose. Meals were more generous and the menu more varied. Now lay men managed the estates for the community, and altogether the professed became an élite group of men little troubled by events in the world outside. The abandonment of their temporal responsibilities to a large group of paid servants – many of whom were sons of the squires and gentry – led to many abuses in the management of the Abbey Manors and estates, and ultimately to the downfall of the monasteries.

John Whitmore, the last Abbot but one, was elected in 1501 and served the Abbey for 28 years. From the records in the P.R.O. (ref. D/L. 3/5, P62, R. 9.), in the year 1508 he was involved in a major upheaval following the death of a freeholder of land on one of the Manors of the Abbey. The deceased left an orphan child which the Abbot took into the custody of his Church and this entitled the Abbot to have custody of the land during the child's minority. It appears however that before his death the father executed a deed of feoffment and a will in favour of John Keynes and Umphrey Walronde, entitling them to take possession of his land. The two gentlemen claimed the child from the custody of the Abbot and entered into possession of the land. A report of the incident sent to the King reads:

... atte your monasterie of Dunkeswell ... diverse wilde gentlemen named John Keynes and Umphrey Walronde gathered a company of riotours to the number of C (100) on horseback and on foote, with bows and arrows, bills and other wepens, made assawte on the Abbot of Dunkeswell, he being within the place, and the Monks att devyn service were sore troubled and greatly abashed, the Abbot seeing their wilde demeanour, called his servants with the other there being with hym, ordeigned for his own defence in the best manner he could to his power, and so had not been for the Visitour of the said Abbey (who was the Abbot of Forde) which then was present, the bothe parties hadde made a grett Fray, but it was letted by the meanes of the said Visitour as God wold ...

A Court of Privy Session was held at Cullompton with a Jury of 12 men to hear the case before which Keynes and Walronde attended with 'frendes and kynnesmen, and there thretaned and manassed the Abbot and said unto hym he should repent it all the daies of his lif if ever the matter came to the King'. Baron Carewe, Justice of the Peace there, and Master More, Justice of Quorum and Custos Rotulorum, entreated the Abbot who was also present, 'desiryng and praying hym to leve his fast and gret labour that he made in this matter, but it was long or thei could dryve hym to lette the matter passe'. When the Abbot agreed 'to leve his suyte and labour' the jury, seeing that '... wolde not fynde nor present the said Riotte'. When the King received a report of the Court of Privy Session he commanded the Bishop of Exeter to enquire into the 'Riotte' and the behaviour of the Justices in dealing with it. The Bishop set up a Courte of Enquiry upon which sat also Robert, Lord Broke, Lewys Pollar Sergeant at Law and John Rowe. When the Abbot was examined he said the story of the riot was untrue and he did not complain to the king nor threaten to do so. The Abbot of Forde was also examined and said:

He saw no riotous demeanour. Keynes asked him to bring peace between the accused and the Abbot of Dunkeswell because of uncourteous words spoken by Keynes and Walronde of the Abbot and the seizure of a ward by the Abbot as the right of his Church, and Keynes and Walronde entering the land of the ward's father on his death by virtue of a will upon a deed of feoffment. Keynes promised to come to the monastery to settle the matter. Keynes and Walronde came with Richard Huggan and Phylyppe Huggan one of the Yeomen of the Crown with servauntes to the number of eight or nine apparelled as gentlemen and their servants out-riding. Does not think they had unlawful wepens. They did not try to hurt the Abbot or other religious person. They talked with the Abbot of Forde for half an hour, drank a cup of wine without speaking to the Abbot of Dunkeswell. Referred case to Council and departed.

Baron Carewe said there was no case put to the Jury of the Court of Privy Session and as there was no proof of the riot the Jury had no findings to make.

The Bishop sent a report of his enquiry to the King and it seems that Abbot Whitmore was adjudged by the King to be at fault as the King granted the Abbot a general pardon for all offences except debt in April 1509. The wardship of an orphan child which had inherited land was the prerogative of the King, who usually appointed a local guardian to take charge of the child and the land. The King had the right to marry off his ward if she was a female to any man of his choice, and there were always a fair number of impoverished courtiers on the look out for the King's favour in such cases. The ward had to accept the husband selected for her by the King or lose her inheritance. It is probable the orphan in this case was a male child, in which case if he was taken into the wardship of the Abbey he would probably have taken vows when he grew up and entered the religious life, when his inheritance would have passed to the Abbey.

The year 1522 was also one of special significance. The Calendar of State Papers (Hen. 8. B16. p1047) reveals that an annual grant of £100 was imposed upon the Abbey for the King's personal expenses in France for the recovery of the Crown. This was a heavy impost which took at least one third of its income and then there were other taxes and the cost of administration to be met from the balance. As the life of the Abbey drew nearer its close financial burdens were increasingly levied upon it by Henry VIII.

The Public Record Office (D/L. 1/4. F3. R2.) records that on 4 May 1522 John Hales, the general Attorney of the King, in the King's Bench, claimed that the Abbot had usurped the King's powers on the Duchy of Lancaster lands held by the Abbey in the Manors of Lincombe, Warcombe, Rapplynghay, Coleton Rale, Donkyswell, Brodehembury, Hawkerlond and Buckland Brewer, which lands John the Abbot held of the King by virtue of Knight's service. The Attorney complained that in these Manors the Abbot had caused the tenants, residents and inhabitants of the Manors to come and appear before the Stewards of the Abbey there, and at the Abbot's Courts Barons he indicted them for misdemeanours, non-observance of manorial customs and dues, and for crimes, and levied fines and amercements upon them and punished for crimes committed within the boundaries of those Manors, all of which, said John Hales, was a usurpation of the King's rights and a disservice to him. The Attorney asked the Court to remedy this situation. Abbot John Whitmore replied saying these powers were confirmed to him by the Justices in Eyre in Court at Exeter on 11 November 1281 by Judge Salomon de Ross and his fellows in regard to the Manors of Buckland Brewer, Lincumbe (of which Warcombe was a part), Broadhembury and Dunkeswell. The land of Hawkerland, said the Abbot, was part of the Manor of Collaton Abbot over which he claimed no jurisdiction, while Rapplynghay was never a Manor nor part of the Duchy of Lancaster. In the Manor of Hackpen the Abbey held similar jurisdiction and these rights were confirmed in 1227 by King Henry III. The Abbot produced the deeds and Charters confirming his entitlement to the powers and the Court later adjourned the case sine die. There were not many Abbots of Religious Houses who held such extensive juridical powers over local populations and who possessed a mandate for the keeping of the King's Peace over such a wide area for three centuries.

The sands of time, however, were running out as the rising tide of nationalism and reformation gathered strength. The corporate life of the Abbey had become stagnant and conservative. The small group of monks led a comfortable life isolated and insulated from the growing storm of hostility in the world outside the precinct. The spiritual life had become tainted with superstition and idolatry and little interest was now taken in temporal affairs, as the management of their Manors and estates were in the hands of paid officials who mostly came from the ranks of the gentry and managed their charges in much the same way as they managed their own private landholdings. The indifference of the monks to the plight of the poor and the sick while at the same time taking the tythes of impropriated churches for themselves gave rise to widespread criticism from the local clergy, who claimed that the tythe taken by the Abbey should be paid to the Church to enable it to fulfil the charitable purposes for which, they said, tythes were paid.

Many influential leaders of the Church were strong advocates for the reform of the Religious Houses, and in 1524 Cardinal Wolsey took steps to dissolve 27 small monasteries, taking their revenues, which totalled £2,300, to found a College at Oxford. The Reformation Parliament of 1529 confirmed the King's break with Rome and established him as Head of the Church in England and this led directly to the destruction of the monasteries, whose allegiance was to Rome. Most of the Religious Houses were the centres of great wealth and the prospect of acquiring this for himself and his depleted Treasury was a strong factor in persuading the King to dissolve the monasteries. There were many Religious Houses well governed and blameless in character but they went down with the many whose life and conduct had become scandalous.

CHAPTER EIGHT

Dissolution of the Abbey

The last Abbot, John Ley, was elected in 1529: he must have known that twilight had descended upon his House and that he was almost certain to be the last of a line of more than 25 Abbots. Shortly after his election, by order of the King, all monks under the age of 24 were expelled from the Abbeys and no man below that age could become a monk. The intake of novices, therefore, was cut off at the source and thus the older monks were not being replaced, so that the number of monks who survived to the dissolution a few years later had fallen to 10. There was also a decline in the number of lay persons serving the Abbey within the walls. The tenants, anxious about their security of tenure if the Abbey was dissolved, took steps to secure from the Abbot an up-to-date lease providing legal entitlement to their holdings. It was well for them that they did this because after the dissolution they were obliged to appear before the Court and to give evidence of legal entitlement to their holdings, without which they were liable to be dispossessed. The Abbot was also charged to produce a detailed statement for the King showing all the sources of income of the Abbey including all rents, the revenues of its Manor Courts and spiritual possessions. The statement when completed was taken to the Bishop of Exeter and in his presence the Abbot was required to declare on oath that it was a true and correct statement and this was certified by the King's Commissioners present for the occasion. The statement was presented on Easter Sunday in the year 1536, just three years before the dissolution of the Abbey. The total net income declared was £294.93p, mainly from 12 Manors and 5 Granges.

Perhaps the most ironic situation that Abbot John Ley found himself in was his appointment by the Bishop in 1537 as one of the last Abbots to act as Collector in Devon of the clerical subsidy to the King. One can imagine the state of turmoil and confusion that must have existed in those religious houses as they awaited the doom that was about to descend upon them. The Lesser Monasteries had been destroyed in 1536 and now had come the turn of the Greater Monasteries, of which Dunkeswell was one. The atmosphere was not conducive to the prompt payment of taxes to the man who had determined to destroy them. Besides, John Ley must have been very fully occupied with the affairs of his own House in preparing for its end which was near at hand. The King, however, was anxious about his money and sent a Commission under his Privy Signet to the Bishop of Exeter commanding him to examine the Collectors of the Clerical subsidy concerning the arrears of those subsidies which should have been paid in to the Bishop of London before the 24 December 1537. The King requested the Bishop to certify to him before the last day of the following February (1538) that he had carried out the terms of the commission and with what result. On the very last day of February 1538 the Bishop and Thomas Brewood (who was probably sent by the King with the Commission) replied to the King saying that the Bishop had summoned every collector of the subsidy, 'commanding them to be with us at Exeter on the 24th of February . . . We know not what the Abbot of Dunkeswell has, for whom we have often sent, but he comes not'. I think we can understand why Abbot John Ley did not come as he was unable to collect much cash, and the winding up of his own House did not leave him much time to travel the County to collect the subsidy from what must have been unwilling payers, so far as the religious houses were concerned.

On 14 February 1539 Abbot John Ley gathered together his small band of ten brethren. It was in the depths of winter and a most depressing time of the year to witness the end of an Abbey that for 338 years had played so outstanding a part in the life and destiny of a large number of people in the eastern region of Devon. This small group, the last of the monks of Dunkeswell, celebrated Mass in their Conventual Church for the last time and then, led by Abbot Ley, they walked to the Chapter House where, after a short prayer, they awaited the arrival of John Tregonwell, the King's Commissioner. In due time, most probably at mid-day, he arrived from the direction of Taunton where he and the other two Commissioners had received the surrender of a number of other religious houses, including William Brewer's foundation of St. John's Hospital at Bridgwater. Tregonwell brought with him a large armed retinue of horsemen who dismounted in the courtyard of the Abbey and prepared themselves for any action they may have been called upon to take if there was resistance to the King's demands for surrender. With his personal assistants Tregonwell entered the Chapter House and sat in the Abbot's seat to receive the community. He demanded that the Abbot and monks should submit to the King's demand and surrender the Abbey and all its possessions. An elaborate instrument of surrender, already drawn up, was read over to the assembled

(signature)	John Ley (Abbot)
(signature)	John Webbe (Steward)
(signature)	John Gaye
(signature)	William Boreman
(signature)	John Segar
(signature)	John Genyng
(signature)	John Benet
(signature)	Thomas Tylsum
(signature)	William Roseter
(signature)	John Hayward

Signatures of the ten monks who signed the deed of surrender to the king of the Cistercian Abbey of Dunkeswell dated 14 February 1539

brethren and this they were requested to sign. To have refused to sign that instrument may well have meant death for the Abbot. The armed men in the courtyard were there to take him prisoner if he refused and the Abbot and brethren were well aware of the fate that had overtaken others who had opposed the surrender of their Houses. The penalty for opposing the King's demand was a charge of treason followed by hanging, drawing and quartering, which not a few Abbots and monks suffered rather than betray the trust of loyalty and the sacred mission of their Order. So John Ley the Abbot, Steward John Webbe and monks John Gaye, William Boreman, John Segar, John Genyng, John Benet, Thomas Tylsum, William Roseter and John Hayward, powerless to do anything else, signed the instrument of surrender. Then followed the handing over of an inventory of all the goods of the Abbey together with all Charters and Seals. The brethren then were ordered off the premises and warned not to return. As they were escorted to the Gatehouse of the Abbey by armed men one can imagine with what heavy hearts they left their home for a hostile world outside.

John Tregonwell and his armed retinue probably remained at the Abbey for a few days and carried out a careful search for rings, vestments of cloth-of-gold and silver and any other items of jewellery or precious stones that may not have been declared in the inventory prepared by the Abbot. It is very probable that they rifled any tombs where they suspected some of these precious objects may have been buried with the dead as it was the custom to do in earlier times. All objects of gold, silver, precious stones and jewellery handed over by the Abbot or found as a result of the search were immediately packed up and despatched post-haste to the King. Having satisfied himself of this John Tregonwell left a small number of armed men to take charge of the surrendered Abbey and its buildings and he with his armed escort went to Canonleigh Abbey, which surrendered two days later on 16 February, and then they passed to Exeter and took the surrender of Polsloe Priory in Heavitree.

At Exeter on 20 February 1539, Tregonwell, Petre and Smyth, the three King's Commissioners in the West, sent a report to Thomas Cromwell, the King's Lord Privy Seal. It reads as follows:

Since last writing have taken the surrender of St. John's in Wells, St. John's in Bridgwater, Athelney, Buckland Monarchum, Tawnton, Dunkiswell, Chanonsleigh and Polsloe, in all of which they have found as much conformity as might be desired except that in many they have found great waste and many leases lately passed which they have stayed and called in again. Having now received the Commission in which Pollard is now joined with them, will divide into two parties and hope thus to make an end before the Annunciation of Our Lady (25th of March) whereby the half year's rent shall remain to the King.

Ask his pleasure touching Bruton and Henton, to the dispatch of which they shall be ready by return of this messenger.

At Exeter 20 February 1539. Signed by the three Commissioners. (Cal. State Papers Hen. 8th Bk 32. V. XIV. Pt. 1. p128).

John Ley was granted a pension of £50 per annum and appointed to the Rectory of Sheldon and Sainthill, and from there in 1556 he went to Payhembury as vicar, where he died a few years later. The Steward of the Abbey (formerly the Cellarer) John Webbe and William Boreman each received an annual pension of £6. John Gaye was appointed to the 'cure' of Sheldon but it would appear that he was either an old or sick man, as provision was made that if he was impotent he was to receive a pension of £5.33p instead of a stipend of £6.67p. John Segar received a pension of £5.33p and John Genyngs, John Benet and Thomas Tylsum each received £4.67p annually, but William Roseter and John Hayward apparently were not awarded pensions. The pensions were worth much less than the amounts stated. They were paid in London half-yearly as a rule which meant that the recipient had to journey to London twice a year to collect them, and this took about three days each way on horseback. A deduction was usually made from the pension by the officials paying it out as a levy or charge for their services. It follows therefore that local pensioners made an arrangement if they could for a local agent to collect the pension for them in return for which he made a charge which was shared by a number of pensioners. In this way the agent often carried a fair sum of money and it was not unknown for him to make off with it or get robbed on the way. In addition, each time a subsidy was granted by Parliament to the King a deduction was made from the pension. So, all in all, it is not surprising that most of the pensioners commuted their pensions for a lump sum, especially those with small pensions where the expense of collecting it was as great almost as the pension itself.

On 4 July 1539 the King granted to John Lord Russell, the President of the King's Council of the West, 'the house and site of the Abbey with the Church, Steeple and Churchyard', a water-mill, gardens, dwellings and woods (400 acres) in Dunkyswylle and Olde Dunkyswylle, the Granges and Bartons of Sheldon, Bowerhayes (362 acres), Bywood, Broadhembury, land at Luppitt and the Parish Churches of Dunkyswylle, Auliscombe and the free Chapel there and the tythes and advowsons estimated by the late Dr. George Oliver at 1,600 acres all told. There were four bells in the tower of the Conventual Church valued at £32.25p and these went to John Russell. Some two years later, on 15 July 1541, John Russell gave back to the King this grant in exchange for land in Lincolnshire, but in the meantime he had sold the fabric of the church and all monastic buildings to John Heydon of Ottery St. Mary for £28 on 27 November 1539. The Indenture providing for the sale included all 'glasse, iron, tymber, stones, tumbe stoneys, or tyle stoneys or paving tyle and all other stuff thyng or thynges being parcell of the said Churche . . . all manner of ledd found or beyng yn or upon the premises only being exempted'. The glass of the lower part of the Cloister and two windows of freestone with the iron of the same were previously sold for the use of 'old Lord Russell'. John Heydon was given ten years in which to pull down, sell and carry away as much as he could. Any treasure found in or about the church by John Heydon and his men during the ten years were to be shared between John Russell and John Heydon, but John Heydon 'shall not have any profit or advantage of any such thyng or thynges as shall chaunce to be found by the said John Heydon withyn any tombe or monyment under the ground withyn the site prsyncke of the said Church and Chauncell'; John Heydon was bound in the sum of £40 to observe this condition.

After stripping the lead from the roof of the church and any other buildings roofed with lead, the remaining buildings were made uninhabitable by damage to the roofs and other parts. Very soon rain, the wind and frost penetrated the inner recesses of the Church and Abbey buildings and in due course nature, as though shocked at the handiwork of the spoiler, spread her mantle of invisibility over the crumbling walls to hide the crime from the eyes of man. What the spoiler did not want from the church he piled up in a great heap outside the western doorway of the church and against the north wall (still standing) of the Cellarer's stores, and there he set fire to the unwanted furnishings of the church and nearby buildings. Until recently the blackened stonework at the base of the north wall of the Cellarer's stores was clear evidence of this great fire.

The remainder of the Abbey land and estates was dispersed between the years 1543–54, and sold off as follows, usually on the basis of 20/21 years purchase of the annual net income:

To Richard Duke of London:
18 July 1543: The Manor of Dotton and the Rectory
of the Chapel of St. Mary. £242.55
Timber in the Woods 33

To Richard Parker of Tavistock:
6 August 1543: The Manor of Lincombe 284.10

To Sir Richard Gresham of London:
7 June 1545: A tenement and garden in Honiton. 8.00

To John Drake of Exeter:
18 March 1545: The Manor of Rapalynghays (Giddesham) 73.85
Timber in the Woods 1.33
The Manor of Weryngeston (Buckerell) 142.71

To John Bourchier, Earl of Bath:
5 September 1545: Hackpen Manor (Uffculme) £722.84
Sheldon and Sainthill Manor 362.41
Bolham Manor (Clayhidon) 273.46
Timber in the Woods 32.84
Spring of the Woods 4.33

To George Rolle and Nicholas Adams:
29 September 1545: The Manor of Buckland Brewer 469.92
Timber in the Woods 9.62
Spring of the Woods 11.67

To Sir George Carew of Exeter:
2 April 1545: The Abbot's House and garden in the
Parish of St. Paul's 1.17

To Edward and Edith Twyhoe and John Watson of More Crichel:
10 March 1546: The Manor of Collaton Abbat (Collaton
    Raleigh)   264.00

To Thomas Goodwin of Plymtree and London:
10 August 1546: Uggaton Manor (Payhembury)   157.58

To the Earl of Southampton, Thos. Wriothesley:
27 February 1548: The Manor of Wolveston (Auliscombe)
    (a gift from the King for an annual rent of £1.27.)   158.15

    The Manor of Broadhembury and Grange. (a gift from
        the King for an annual rent of £6.) Worth   £1,062.58

To Giles Keyleway and William Leonard of Taunton:
2 August 1549: The Rectory of Sheldon and Sainthill.   13.33

To the Marchioness Gertrude of Exeter:
24 October 1553: The Manor of Hawkerlond (Collaton
    Raleigh).   238.00

To Elizabeth Grosvenor of London:
22 June 1545: The Manor of Shabbecombe (Luppitt).   221.04

                    Total value of Abbey estates.   £4,755.81

Land remaining in possession of the King after 1558:
The Manor of Dunkeswell. Assessed Rents.   19.94

    Farm of the Abbey site. The Grange of Bowerhayes, a water-mill and three
parts of a meadow in Shabbcombe in the Parish of Luppitt.   23.00

New rents from John Gennynge (a former Monk) and
    John Mitchell.   13
Court Profits, including £1.30p for heriots   1.62
Farm of the Grange of Bywood.   11.00

                                             £55.69
 ("Devon Monastic Lands"
  by Joyce Youings B.A.   Less £2 for the Bailiff   2.00
  Ph.D. Dev. & Cornwall
  Record Society. Vol. 1.   Net rents   £53.69

The residue of Abbey land was administered from Bowerhayes Grange by a
Crown Bailiff down to the late 18th century when what was left of it passed
into the possession of the Wolford Estate.

    As time passed the Abbey became a quarry from which stones were taken to
build farmhouses and cottages in the neighbourhood, and a close scrutiny of

some of their walls will reveal carved and dressed stone that once was part of the Abbey structures. Some remains were gradually adapted for use as cottages, shelters and sheds for people and animals who occupied them for at least two centuries. Most of the stones which remained in the early years of the 19th. century were used to erect the Holy Trinity Church in 1842 upon a part of the site of the Nave of the Conventual Church, the east burial ground of which embraces the site of the Lady Chapel. What now remains of the Abbey is a part of the gatehouse and some outer walls of the Cellarer's store. Some of the occupied buildings around the vicinity of the site are undoubtedly part of the Abbey structures adapted for occupation, and the foundations lie below ground.

Some ten years after the erection of Holy Trinity Church, on 2 June 1852, a workman driving his horse-and-cart over a cleared portion of the Abbey remains, where the ground became scorched in dry summers, noticed a hollow sound and taking his mattock he uncovered two stone coffins with signs of the burial of a child between them. The coffins were lifted and found to contain the remains of a man and a woman. The remains were placed together in one of the coffins and reburied in consecrated ground at a point south-east of the church and in a corner spot formed by the junction of the south wall and a short wall running north. The other coffin was placed over the spot to mark it but, after remaining there for some 60 years, it was brought into the church in 1914, where it now lies. The remains discovered were very probably those of a benefactor of the Abbey and his wife who were buried in or near the Chapter House in the 13th. century.

Dunkeswell Abbey: one of two stone coffins discovered on the site of the Chapter House on 29 June 1852. The burial took place in the thirteenth century and contained the remains of a man and a woman – perhaps a benefactor of the abbey and his wife

Holy Trinity Church, Dunkeswell Abbey, consecrated 21 September 1842. It was built on part of the site of the Conventual Church with stone from the ruins of the abbey

The last remaining corbel, showing the face of a former abbot

North-east corner of the Gatehouse, with remains of the newel stairs on the left

Doorway from the lower chamber of the Gatehouse giving access to the newel stairs and chamber above

The doorway at the top of the newel stairs giving access to the upper chamber

North wall of the cellarer's range. Note thickness of walls

Residents outside their home in an abbey ruin, from a Simcoe sketch of
c. 1840

𝕶𝖓𝖔𝖜𝖓 𝕬𝖇𝖇𝖔𝖙𝖘 𝖔𝖋 𝕯𝖚𝖓𝖐𝖊𝖘𝖜𝖊𝖑𝖑

1219 (before)	William	Cartulary of Canonsleigh No. 62. p21.
1228–33	Richard	Land purchased from Richard de Crues. Close Rolls Hen. III Bk. 2. p295.
1238	John	Devon Fete of Fines 559.
1249–51	Ralph	Translation to Waverley Abbey and Devon Fete of Fines 462.
1253–56	Thomas	Lease and Devon Fete of Fines 559.
1259	John	Wriothesley Deed 66 Hampshire R.O.
1275	John	Devon Fete of Fines Vol. 2. No. 779.
1311–18	John	Bishop Stapleton's Registers.
1318–21	William	Wriothesley Deed 48 Hampshire R.O. and Episcopal Registers.
1321–29	William de Wanlake	Episcopal Registers. Close Rolls Bk. 19. Edw. III.
1341	John	Dr. George Oliver's Monasticon 1846.
1341–46	Simon	Blessed by the Bishop Feb. 22nd and Oliver's Monasticon 1846.
1346–48	John de Wallis	The Cellarer from Newenham Abbey. Elected 22nd April 1346. Close Rolls Bk. 26 Edw. III.
1353	William Wedmore	Succeeded April 7th. Episcopal Reg.
1378	Richard	Close Rolls Bk. 33. Richard II.
1382–97	Robert Orchard	Episcopal Registers.
1397–99	Alexander Burlescombe	Episcopal Registers.
1399–21	Richard Lamport.	Episcopal Registers and Patent Rolls Bk. 80. p228.
1419–38	John Bokeland	Elected 10 June 1419 but the death of the Bishop in September deferred for 2 years his confirmation. Episcopal Reg.
1439–69	John Otery	Episcopal Registers.
1470	William	Wriothesley Deed 62. Hampshire R.O.
1474–89	Thomas Dulton	Leases and Oliver's Monasticon.

119

1492–98	Richard Pytmynster	Leases and Oliver's Monasticon.
1501–29	John Whitmore	Leases.
1529–39	John Ley	Leases and Deed of Surrender.

Some Abbots officiated for longer periods than the dates suggest and although we can account for 25 Abbots there are probably a few more at present unknown.

Tenancy Leases

Granted by the Abbots of Dunkeswell
1465–1538

Taken from a manuscript at Powderham Castle, near Exeter, by the late Dr. George Oliver in 1825, they are believed to have come from the Exchequer Augmentation Office records of the Abbey acquired by them after the dissolution in 1539 and used by their representatives at Exeter for the purpose of identifying tenants in connection with the sale and disposal of Abbey lands. About 180 leases are listed and they represent about 77 per cent. of the rents in the Parishes listed, and about 64 per cent. of the total rents from all sources.

PARISH OF AULISCOMBE:

Barton of Auliscombe:
Serle, John and 2 others, 1481, land called Pouley and Fotelonde, Lease renewed by the Abbot in 1496. Rent 59p.
Serle, John, Thomas and Jane, 1535, a tenement in the Parish. Rent £2.47½p.
Wolveston Manor:
Serle, John and 2 others, 1481, a tenement in Colehege. Rent 33p.
Serle, William, 1485, a tenement with common pasture. Rent 27p
Chanon, Christopher and 2 others, 1535, a tenement. Rent £1.33p.
Dunn, John, 1523, reversion of an estate held by John Leyng and reversion of William Husey's tenement. Rent 33p.
Husey, William and 3 others, 1518, a tenement in Colehege formerly held by John Serle above. Rent 33p.
Husey, William and Margaret his wife, 1509, another property. Rent 82p.
Harryes, Stephen for life, 1521, a tenement, Rent 37p.
Northampton, John and his 2 sons, 1534, an estate. Rent 50p. (The Abbey Bailiff for the Manor).
Northampton, William on 3 lives, 1534, a tenement and premises in Colehege. Rent 67p.
Serle, Jane and 2 others, 1535, a tenement. Rent 27p.

PARISH OF BROADHEMBURY:
Manor of Broadhembury:
Boucher, John and 3 of the family, 1535, a cottage, garden and part of Bremelond Barton with cottage and appurtenances in the Parish. Rent 95p.
Butt, Robert and wife, 1510, a tenement and part of Estfylde Barton. Rent £1.72p.
Butt family, 1525, (of 4 members), a tenement at Estfylde Barton. Rent 80p.
Harding, Robert and 3 others, 1534, cottage and part of a meadow in the village, also part of Legh Barton with a barn and some premises in that village. Rent £1.53p.
Hardynge, William and 2 others, 1495, 2 cottages with Shapcrofts, Bowode and part of a

meadow near the water, also a close called Le More and pasture in Hemburycombe and Downes. Rent 85p.

Hardynge, Alice widow and 2 others, 1536, the reversion of the above on the death of her husband William. Rent 85p.

Rugge family for 3 lives, 1496, a cottage and appurtenances and land called Comepark, Solashayspark, Outland, Solashayspit, also a cottage at Luppitt. Rent £1.10p.

Rugge, Thomas and 3 lives, 1529, reversion of the above tenancy at a rent of £1.20p.

Salter, Thomas and 2 others, 1532, reversion of a cottage and £1 at Michaelmas (29th September) in lieu of labour for the Abbot in the Autumn.

Wilcote, John and 3 others, 1533, a cottage and right of common. Rent 40p.

Wolnesley, John and 5 lives, 1533, two farms and pasture on Hemburycombe and Downe and Coleton More, heriot the best beast and to reap the corn 10 days in the Autumn for the Abbot. Rent 67p.

Woodland, John and 3 others, 1533, a tenement and Newmore 4 acres, Moreland 2 acres, Okehills 5 acres, Rugwaylane 4 acres, Langpark 5 acres, also 6 acres on the West side of Whitehills, 4 acres called Longmede, Speremede, Tadwill and Litelsowe, a parcel called Pondmede and orchard and a croft. Rent 53p.

No name. 1534, a tenement called Hanger for 4 lives. Rent 67p.

Richard, Stephen and 3 others, 1537, a tenement in Le Breton. (Legh Barton) Rent 45p.

Coleton: (or Colyton).

Taylor, John for life, 1465, a tenement called West Place. Rent 24p.

Taylor, Thomas and 2 others, 1533, reversion of the above tenancy at the same rent.

Gent, Thomas and 2 others, 1484, a tenement with a Water Mill called Froggmille and all its business as also the piece of land called the Myll Place. Rent £1.03p.

Hayes, William For 3 lives, 1530, reversion of the above tenancy at the same rent.

Bowden, John and 2 others, 1536, a cottage and land. 50p Rent.

Bowden, Family for 2 lives, 1533, a cottage. Rent 17½p.

Facye, John, 1521, an estate held by his family before. Rent 40p.

Smyth, Catherine and 3 others, 1524, a tenement and right of pasture on Colyton More, Hemburycombe and Downe. Rent 50p.

Potter family, 1527, the above tenancy taken over from the Smyth family at the same rent.

Whiteway, Edward and 2 others, 1533, a tenement with Millonde, Northdon, Whithill, Rispark, Southmede, Estmede, Broadpark, Meyfordlonde, Litelshade, Fouracres, Croftspark, Waterletts. Rent £1.67p.

Loveton:

Lane, Jane and Thomas for their lives, 1521, two tenements Rent 67p.

Lanes for 3 lives, in addition to the above, some other property in Loveton also 6p instead of 15 days labour for the Abbot in the Autumn besides 1p at Michaelmas, 1532. Rent £1.66p.

Skynner, Richard and 2 others, 1534, a tenement and part of the lands of Morden Barton. Rent 45p.

Cranmore:

Wallysleigh, Nicholas for life, 1484, a tenement in Cranmore. Rent 22½p.

Cutforthe, Alice and William Warryn of Landford, 1530, reversion of the above tenancy at the same rent.

Parkyn, William and 5 of the family, 1489, the reversion of two tenements. Rents 60p.

Elys family, 1497, reversion of some property. Rent 60p.

Segar, Jane, 1527, an estate called Pound in Cranmore for 80 years. Rent 65p.

Hyll, John and 3 others, 1534, reversion of the estate called Pound in Cranmore and right of pasture on Coleton More. Rent 67p.

Trumpe, John and one more, 1538, a tenement called Overplace. Rent 22p.

Stowford:

Werthe, John and 3 of the family, 1474, two tenements. Rent for Lewys tenancy 54p and for Smyth tenancy 24p.

Pitt, Robert who had married a daughter of Werthe and to 3 of the children, 1522, the estate above. Rent increased to £1.

Northampton, William and 2 others, 1531, part of the Barton called Mollyshille and a tenement in Broadhembury. Rent £2.

Mutter, Thomas and 2 more of the family, 1534, a cottage. Rent 60p.

Mutters family, of 4, the above lease renewed with the right of pasture, 1538.

Cutford, Thomas and his 2 sons, 1533, reversion of a tenement. Rent 25p.

Upcote:

Elys, John and 2 others, 1497, some property in Upcote besides 15p for the field called Rymedepark. Rent £1.10p.

Beauford, Thomas, 1501, reversion of Rymede and Tronteryslond. Rent 25p.

Perkyns, 1501, a tenement and 6 acres in Upcote. Rent 70p.

Tose family, 1532, reversion of 2 tenements Rymede and Tronteryslond for 3 lives. Rent £1.26p.

Wilnerley, John and 4 others, 1534, a tenement called Overplace in Upcote and 1½ acres in New-more. Rent 25p.

Stremer, Alice widow for her life, no date, a tenement in Upcote of 12 acres of land and a virgate (30 acres) of meadow. Rent 65p.

Stremer, Robert and Agnes, 1535, the reversion of the above estate. Rent 65p.

Potter family, 1538, for 98 years some cottages and land called Bremlond and Redehill. Rent £1.90p.

Uggaton Manor: (Payhembury Parish included in Broadhembury).

Markur, Ibota widow, no date, part of Brodeley Barton for life. Rent 75p.

Markur family, of 4 in 1524 granted the reversion of the above at the same rent.

Potter family, of 2, 1511, part of Brodeley Barton with right of pasture on Ugdowne and Closedowne. Rent £1.

Salter, Joan widow and John At Fen, Orehill and a tenement in Uggaton. Rent £1.50p.

Skynner, William and 2 others, 1535, an estate and two closes called Bromepark and Southwater. Rent £3.38p.

PARISH OF BUCKERELL:

Weryngstone Manor:

Haye, John for life, 1498, a tenement in Westryngston in the Parish of Buckerell. Rent 40p.

Strete, John for life, no date, 19½ acres of land at Weryngston and Rapalynhayes with pasture upon all the 'montem' (Hill) of Giddesham.

Apryse, William, Margaret his wife and Mary his daughter, 1526, the above tenancy lately occupied by John Strete. Rent £1.

Apryse, William above and 2 others, 1526, a tenement in Weryngston Manor in Buckerell and right of pasture on Giddisham Hill. Rent 50p.

Waryn, John and 3 lives, 1516, 2 tenements in the Manor. The lease renewed at the same rent in 1531 to John Waryn and 3 lives. Rent £1.20p.

Caunt, John and 2 others, 1521, a tenement in Weryngston. Rent 60p.

Flaye, John, his wife Margaret and their sons John and George, 1535, the tenement and estate in Weryngston lately held by John Flaye deceased. Rent £2.49p.

PARISH OF CLAYHIDON:

Bolham Manor:

Browne, Robert for 3 lives, 1497, the close called Haselbeare Park, 3 acres of land called Haselbearemede and Haselberewood. Rent £1.13p.

Taylor, Richard and 2 others, 1521, a close called Bolhamfyld. Rent 67p.

Tucker, Thomas and 2 others, 1521, land called Littleshade with Colehaymede and a lane called Littleshadoway. Heriot 50p. (Bailiff of the Manor) Rent 50p.

The reversion of the above to 3 of the daughters of Thomas and *Wilmote Tucker*, 1533, the rent increased to £1.12p.

Pococke, John of Olde Dunkeswell and his eldest son, 1533, the lease for lives of Langham. Rent 67p.

Phillips, John (senior) and 2 others, 1533, Bolham Hurst and Longmede, and pannage and mastage in bosco of Riggewood. (Means the right of feeding swine on acorns, beech mast, chestnuts etc., on the wooded slopes of Riggewood) Rent 80p.

London, Robert, 1537, for 70 years an estate at Bolham. Rent £1.22p.

Buckland Roche:

Boby, John, 1539, farm of a messuage by Indenture. Rent £2.67p.

PARISH OF DUNKESWELL:

Olde Dunkeswell:

Harryes, Stephen, 1521, reversion of Morelesshayes for life. Rent 45p.

Onanleigh, John and 2 others, 1532, a tenement called Sendcomer and some land called Le Strete on the north side of the tenement and land called Jameswood on the West side. Rent 67p.

Phillips, John and 3 others, 1534, the estate called Southpoyd, rent 40p and Northpoyd, rent 67p for their lives.

Phillips, Robert and 2 of his family, 1538, the Corn Mill and appurtenances. Rent 27p.

Serle, Agnes and 3 others 1532, reversion of a tenement and a field called Fotelond. Rent 27p.

Smythe, Jane and 3 others, 1533, lease of Tencery and some other land in the Parish. Rent 50p.

Bowerhayes Manor:

Beche, John and 2 others, 1530, a tenement called Swyttekaishaie. Rent £1.

Browne, John before 1536, an estate in Bowerhayes. Rent 20p.

Chanon, Christopher and 2 others, 1537, a close called 'Uttersouthayes'. Rent 20p.

Ley, Henry, son of Alice Ley deceased, 1538, a tenement with Stonifylde and right of pasture, for 98 years. For tenement 90p, for Stonifyledmede 33p.

Phillips, John Junior, 1537, Pitplace and Rufgreylonde with right of pasture for 70 years. Rent £1.

Phillips, Thomas, 1538, estate in Bowerhayes which was tenanted by Robert Chanon. To hold for 90 years. Rent £1.17p.

Pococke, John, 1508, two tenements and one cottage at Huntshayes. Rent £1.

Serle, John and 3 others, 1511, lease of Western Southayes. Rent 60p.

Serle, William and 2 others, 1537, an estate at Southayes. Rent 60p.

Taylor, Richard and 3 others, 1538, a tenement for life. Rent 67p.

Toker, John and 2 others, 1536, an estate occupied by John Browne. Rent 20p.

Wulferchurche Manor:

Prynge, William and 3 others, 1496, an estate at Wullforde Church. Rent 55p.

Prynge, Robert and Agness, 1536, reversion of the above estate on the death of William Prynge. Rent 55p.

Serle, Jane and 2 others, 1531, a close at Wolferchurche also the "More" there. Rent £2.13p.

The Grange:

Serle, John, Thomas and Jane of Wolveston, 1535, the Grange called Wolferchurche. Rent £6.33p.

PARISH OF LUPPITT:

Shabbcombe Manor:

Horewood, Henry, Jane and Andrew, 1494, the capital messuage of Shabbcombe for their lives. Heriot the best beast or chattels or the value at the option of the Abbot and Convent. The 'fine' (or premium) for the lease was £4.35p (two years rent). The farm or Grange had been managed by a Bailiff for the Abbey but was now leased to a tenant for rent with the live and dead stock on the land. Rent £2.18p.

Brome, John and 2 others of his family, 1538, three tenements in Shabbcombe and land called

Stikildowne, Longland, Gawlemore, Twelveacres and Little Greylondsmede. Rent £1.08p.

Lambert, John and 3 others, 1531, reversion of some land. Rent 83p.

Menyse family, Robert, Jane and Thomas, 1493, reversion of an estate then held by Bennet Hygons with another called Whitemede, for their lives. Rent £1.63p.

Menyse family, for 3 lives, the above lease renewed in 1533, the estate being described as Trapill's lond and Wilkeslond with a grove. Rent £1.63p.

Mewer, William and 2 others, 1501, the reversion of Mordehill and Bokehyshays, Hinkesclyffe and Epyddhe in Shabbcombe. Rent £1.18p.

Phillips, John, 1531, a meadow for 3 lives. Rent 13p.

Phillips, John and 3 others, 1534, the meadow called Hadderley near Greylondesfote. Rent 27p.

Rugge, Thomas and 3 lives, 1529, a cottage with Greylondsmede, Prest, Myllwood and a small meadow adjoining also Symonscroft. Rent 60p.

PARISH OF GIDDESHAM:

Manor of Rapalynghey:
Vowler, Agnes, Widow and her sons Christopher and George, 1525, the estate lately occupied by her husband Nicholas, for their lives. Heriot the best beast. Common pasture is granted on the whole Mount of Giddisham. Rent £3.17p.

Sherman, John, before 1536, a free rent. 2p.

BURGO DE HONYTON:

Tryppe, John and Joan his wife and their children John and Mary, 1533, a tenement and garden being near Catherine Carew's heirs on the West and the estate of the heirs of William Courtnay called Le Place on the East, rent £1, also 2 acres of land in Buckerell Parish, rent 13p for their lives.

PARISH OF SHELDON:

Sheldon Manor:
Baker, John and 2 others of the family, 1530, Northweylonde, Clampatlonde and Prutteshays in the Manor. Rent 40p.

Knyght, Robert and Jane for life, 1514, Prustylonde and Prustmore in Shildon Manor. Rent 35p.

Knyght, John and 2 others, 1531, a tenement at Slade with Pitlond in Shildon Manor. Rent for tenement 32p, for Pitlond 15p, 'pro auxilio' (feudal aid) 3p and "pro Hundred manspenny" (a local tax) 1p.

Tye family, before 1528, an estate with a 'More' there lately enclosed. Rent £1.33p.

Somerhayes, William and 2 others, 1528, the above estate between Carteryshlonde and Pitlonde in Shildon Parish and Olde Dunkeswell once occupied by the Tye family. Rent £1.33p.

Northcote:
Blackmore, John and son, 1535, 2 tenements and land called Langlegh in Shildon. Rent 55p.

Westcote:
Hill, Walter and his wife Matilda for life, 1509, two tenements. Rent 55p.

Hill family, above, 1528, a tenement in Westcote for three lives. Rent 33p.

Donne, John and 2 others, 1535, a property, rent 33p.

Sholashe, John and 2 others, 1536, two tenements. The lease renewed again by the Abbot 11–9–1537. Rent 55p.

The Grange Sheldon:
Stowford, William for 60 years, 4–9–1535, with 2 closes called Hockedrise and Cradcombe and pasture on Colewoodedown, Sheldon Downe and Dunkeswell Downe, lessee to do repairs. The Grange was formerly managed directly by the Abbey. William Stowford was the Auditor of all the premises of the Abbey. Rent £5.03p.

PARISH OF KENTISBEARE:

Sainthill:
Smith, John 1484, a close called Abbeysfyld near Morelpen and the land of Sainthill with appurtenances for life. Rent £1.30p.
Grene, John and Jane and their son, a reversion of the above property. Rent £1.30p. 18–6–1484.
Slade, Margaret and 2 others, 1526, land called Saynthilford with 2 meadows adjoining also a field called Hearynge in Kentisbeare with right of pasture. Rent £1.33p.

PARISH OF UFFCULME:

Manor of Smythencote:
Hogge, John and 2 others, 1492, an estate in the Manor. Rent 25p.
Manor of Hackpen:
Dionysia, John and John Rigge, 1512, two tenements, one called Atterhill at Hackpen. Rent 83p.
Leyman, Robert and Elizabeth, 1492, certain property not described but previously directly managed by the Abbey. Rent 98p.
Layman, Robert for 90 years, 1538, a tenement in Hackpen and 3 closes called Stopehyll. Rent £2.15p.
Marshall, Richard and his 2 sons, 1532, a meadow called Duckmede near Hackpen Mill with land called Langlond formerly tenanted by John Sydenham, Gent. Rent for Duckmede 26p, for Langlond 60p.
Pepperell, John and Isabella his wife and 2 others, 1534, an estate in Hackpen lately tenanted by Richard Williams, also Bromefields and Estlanglonde there. Rent £1.12p.
Pococke, John and 2 sons, 1535, the estate of Downeland in Hackpen. Rent 35p.
Sydenham, Thomas, Gent., 1536, a Corn Mill at Hackpen with a fulling Mill adjoining and its appurtenances. Rent 60p. (He was Steward of the Abbey at this time).
Craddock: (Hackpen Manor):
Marshall, William for life, 1477, a tenement in Cradocke with right of pasture and timber for repairs etc., from Colewood and Eggewood. Rent 23p.
Marshall family, of 3, the Abbot renews the above lease in 1533 at the same rent.
Campany, John and 2 others, 1536, a tenement in Cradocke with Frenchmede near Hackpen Mill. Rent 62p.
Cole, John and 2 others, 1532, part of Cradocke estate with Frenchmede. Rent 33p.
Dowdenay, Robert and 3 others of the family, 1538, two tenements and a Fulling Mill in Cradocke. Heriot 'duo meliora averia' (two good cattle). Rent 51p.
Garswell, Robert, his wife and son, 1530, an estate at Cradocke. Rent 67p.
Mylle, Robert and 2 others, 1523, a tenement in Cradocke, a meadow called Brigemede, the Corn Mill near the 'Buddell' (a trough, probably timbered, set in the water course of Hackpen Mill and most likely used for sheep washing). Rent for tenement 23p, for the meadow 25p and for the Mill 13p.
Mylle, Robert and 3 others, 1533, the whole estate of Cradocke. Rent 77p.
Mylle, John and 2 others, 1531, an estate at Cradocke. Rent 77p.
Northampton, John and 2 others, 1529, an estate in Cradocke and pasture upon Hackpen Hill. Rent 50p.
Prynge, Thomas and 2 others, 1538, two estates in Cradocke. Rent 52p.
White, John and 2 others, 1532, a tenement and some land adjoining in Cradocke. Rent 33p.
Northcote (Hackpen Manor):
Walleronde, William Esq., 1486, 3 tenements at Northcote and some land called Haywood for 70 years. Rent 87p.
Baker, Nicholas and 2 others, 1533, a tenement and some premises in Northcote, Hackpen. Rent £1.35p.
Bashley, William and 2 sons, 1537, a premium of £2 was paid for the reversion of 3 tenements at La More, Northcote, near Cradocke in the Manor of Hackpen and Bruggemede was its 4

ditches, also a garden at La More, also Slademede with the right of pasture on Hackendowne for lives. Rent of tenements 67½p, for Bruggemede 15p, for the garden 3p and for Slademede 40p.
Cregan, William and 3 others of the family, 1535, a tenement and some land called Chaldfild and 2 closes called Stapehill at Northcote in Hackpen Manor. Rent for tenement 27½p, for Chaldfield 13p, for Stapehill 44p.
Goodrigge, Florence and 2 others, 1535, an estate in Northcote in Hackpen. Rent 36p.
Knolles, John and 3 others, 1531, 3 tenements at La More at Northcote near Cradcocke, also Brigmede, also a garden at La More also Slademede. Rent £1.26p. (see Bashley above).
Marchall, John, 1477, a cottage in Mochylfylde in Norcote, Hackpen Manor. Rent 96p.
Marshall family, for 3 lives, 1517, the Abbot renewed the lease of the above tenancy at the same rent.
Oteway, Jane widow and Robert, Jane and Anthony Oteway, 1537, for their lives, a tenement in Northcote, Hackpen. Rent 29p.
Ashill, Hackpen Manor:
Broke, Alice and 2 others, 1533, property not described. A tenement rent 66p, for some land 8p, towards repairing the Mill stream besides 13p more.
Baker, Robert and 3 of his family, 1534, two tenements in Ashill and another tenement with some land in Umbrook within the Manor of Hackpen. Rent £1.02p.
Broke, John and 2 others, 1534, a tenement and some land at Ashill, Hackpen. Rent £1.25p.
Cole or Karswill, Richard and 2 others, 1535, an estate in Ashill. Rent 30p.
Dunn, John labourer and 2 others, 1533, a tenement in Ashill at Hackpen for their lives. Rent 50p.
Hogge, John, his wife and 2 sons, 1532, an estate in Ashill, Hackpen. Rent £1.
Layman, John and 2 others, 1498, property in Ashill also Halond and Haymede. Rent 90p.
Layman family, some of them, 1533, the Abbot renews the above lease at the same rent.
Marshall, Richard and 3 others, 1533, 2 tenements in Wombroke (Umbroke) in Hackpen Manor and pasture upon Hackpen Hill. Rent 67p.
Whitemore, Robert and his son John, 1521, the estate in Ashill, Hackpen Manor that had been occupied by Catherine the mother of the said Robert. Rent 50p.
Rull, Hackpen Manor:
Goodriche, Alice and her 2 sons, 1532, 2 tenements in Rille (Rull) and one close called Umbroke in Hackpen Manor. Rent 75p.
Goodridge, John and 3 others, 1533, the estate at Rille (Rull) in Hackpen. Rent £1.50p.
No name, 1527, reversion of a cottage and lands at Trell (Rull) also a close called Le Parke in Hackpen for 3 lives, Rent for cottage and lands 98p and for Le Parke 60p.
Leynor: (Leigh–Hackpen Manor):
Woodbury, John, farm of a messuage with land appurtaining and leased sometime before 1536. Rent £2.

PARISH OF COLLATON RALEIGH:

Coleton Abbat:
Hoppyn, Roger and 2 others, 1522, a tenement also land adjoining, Rent for tenement 40p, for land 55p.
Oliver, Richard and Jane his wife and Maurice their son, 1525, a tenement in Coleton and Wormelyff Mill. The Abbot to provide "lapides molares" (grinding stones) and sufficient 'estakespro les hedware' (timber for the millstream) from his woods in Hawkerlonde. Rent 75p.
Page, John and 2 others, 1531, on lives, Wormeclyffillikin at Collaton Abbot. Rent £1.55p.
Hawkerlond Manor:
Elliot, Alexander for 3 lives, 1526, an estate in the Manor. Rent £1.
Kingeston:
Elyot, Alexander and 3 others, 1526, a tenement in Kingeston in the Parish of Collaton Raleigh. Rent £1.01p and a cottage there 40p. Heriot 25p.

Dotton:

Stowford, William and Beatrice his wife and sons John and Walter, 20–7–1532, farm of the Chapel revenues. Rent £1.

PARISH OF CHERITON FITZPAINE:

Lake, William, before 1538, a tenement. Rent 25p.

CITY OF EXETER:

Parish of St. Paul's:
Mawdit, Richard, 1532, the garden of the Abbot's House for a term of 58 years. The said Richard within five years to build a new house upon the garden. Rent 13p.
(These entries were taken from the typescript copies in the Exeter City Library).

DESMESNE LANDS OF THE ABBEY:

In proper tenure of the Abbot 1536:

Broadhembury Grange fixed rents	£12.00p.
Bywood Grange	3.33p.
Bowerhayes Grange	7.50p.
Sheldon Grange	4.00p.
Shabbcombe, lands at	2.85p.
Dunkeswyll with the Corn Mill	5.00p.

Net income £34.68p.

SPIRITUAL POSSESSIONS:

From the Impropriated Churches – Annual Tythes:

AULISCOMBE: Rectory worth in common years in tythe of sheaves (corn). £9.00p.
DOTTON: Free Chapel there worth in tythe. 1.30p.
OLDE DUNKESWYLL: Rectory worth in tythe of sheaves £1.33p
wool and lambs £1.18p and Personal (from craftsmen serving the Abbey). Less payments
to the Diocese. 5.26p.
SHELDON: Rectory worth in tythe of sheaves £1.33p, of wool, lambs and
calves £1.18p, other tythes and oblations as appear in the Paschali Book £1.28p. 3.51p.

£19.07p.

Index

129